The California Tomorrow Plan

# The California Tomorrow Plan

Edited by Alfred Heller

WILLIAM KAUFMANN, INC.    LOS ALTOS, CALIFORNIA

Task force for

## THE CALIFORNIA TOMORROW PLAN revised edition

ALFRED HELLER, *chairman and plan editor; president, California Tomorrow, San Francisco*

JOHN W. ABBOTT, *executive secretary and editor, California Tomorrow*

WILLIE L. BROWN, JR., *member, California State Assembly, 18th District*

SIMON EISNER, *planning consultant, Simon Eisner & Associates, South Pasadena*

THEODORE FOIN, *assistant professor of environmental studies, University of California, Davis*

MARC E. GOLDSTEIN, *general partner in design, Skidmore, Owings & Merrill, San Francisco*

NATHANIEL A. OWINGS, *Skidmore, Owings & Merrill, San Francisco*

VICTOR H. PALMIERI, *principal, Victor Palmieri/Bruce Juell and Company, Los Angeles*

HARVEY S. PERLOFF, *dean, school of architecture and urban planning, University of California, Los Angeles*

WILLIAM M. ROTH, *San Francisco*

FRANK M. STEAD, *environmental consultant, Piedmont*

KENNETH E. F. WATT, *professor of zoology and systems ecologist, University of California, Davis*

SAMUEL E. WOOD, *planning consultant, Sacramento*

*Editorial Assistants*

RUTH HELLER
CHERYL BRANDT
STEPHEN WHITNEY
ALICE ADAMS
CHARLOTTE GEHRET
JEAN FORTNA
STEVEN GOLDMAN
GREGORY MARRONE
FRANI CHIAPPETTA
KAY SMITH

CREDITS

*Cover and book design:* WOLFGANG LEDERER
*Production supervision; maps and charts:* JOHN BEYER
*Drawings:* JOHN KRIKEN

Printed on recycled paper

# Publisher's Foreword

THE CALIFORNIA TOMORROW PLAN is our first book. We believe it is an important book, one which has profound implications that will be apparent to everyone who reads it carefully. It addresses itself effectively and in an innovative way not only to our most pressing environmental problems but also to related social and economic imbalances in our society. Most significantly, it emphasizes problem-solving and offers specific, workable, constructive programs of action.

The book was developed by California Tomorrow, a nonprofit educational organization formed in 1961 by a group of California citizens with the conviction "that the work and activities of man should and can be so ordered that all citizens of the state may continually enjoy the widest variety of choice environment, including quiet and light, pure air and water, and a fair share of untrammeled green earth." California Tomorrow has dedicated itself to illuminating the problems we must solve and the courses we might follow to maintain California as a beautiful and productive state. A constant theme of its publications, including the award-winning quarterly journal, *Cry California*, has been the urgent need for comprehensive statewide planning.

In 1970 California Tomorrow initiated the development of long-overdue, systematic plans for the future of the people, lands and cities of California. A task force of leaders was assembled from architectural, agricultural, environmental, economic, engineering, health, social and urban planning, and other special fields to help California Tomorrow formulate and design a model of what comprehensive state planning could be and could accomplish. *The California Tomorrow Plan—A First Sketch*, published in March 1971 in tabloid newspaper format, attracted widespread attention throughout the United States and in many foreign countries. Reactions came from public officials, the news media, teachers and interested individuals, demonstrating a strong public interest in the planning process as a means of finding practical solutions to society's increasingly complex problems. A thorough revision of the plan was then undertaken, utilizing these reactions and other suggestions for improving and refining it, and it now becomes available for the first time in book form.

THE CALIFORNIA TOMORROW PLAN represents a unique attempt by a group of individuals in this state to assert some constructive influences on the course of events. Thus it is a particularly appropriate first offering from a new California-based publisher. Furthermore, the earliest books that appear under a publisher's imprint are important to the publisher himself, for they stand as his introduction to the world at large. They represent some of his major concerns and interests and hopes for the future. Among our immediate objectives is the publication of other broadly conceived, interdisciplinary studies. We trust that our subsequent offerings will confirm our deep and abiding interest in the whole earth and the myriad life forms and styles it nurtures and supports.

We hope the citizens of many states and countries will read THE CALIFORNIA TOMORROW PLAN and discover in it not only food for thought but also encouragement to initiate and support the kinds of comprehensive planning that are urgently needed in their own regions. Although the plan described in this book focuses primarily on California, we are confident that its applications are universal.

We look forward to our readers' comments and suggestions.

WILLIAM KAUFMANN

# Contents

Dedicated to
the children of California

# Introduction

## A new kind of planning

This is a plan for California—its land, its cities and its people. It shows how the people of California can deal in a systematic, constructive way with the state's most serious problems; and it predicts the results of following such a course—new opportunities for personal initiative and fulfillment, and a healthful environment for everyone.

The achievement of such results will, indeed, take planning—not alone "land-use" planning or "social" planning or "economic" planning or "architectural" planning, but a new kind of **comprehensive** planning which is highly responsive to the needs of people and the portion of the planet they occupy.

Consider the continuing warfare between conservation groups on the one hand and labor and business interests on the other. The California Tomorrow Plan offers a specific alternative to this kind of dangerous civil war—a single, easily understood set of policies and goals by which we can solve our most critical problems. By contrast, public policy seldom takes into account the inseparable connection of economic and social programs with those that aim to protect the natural environment. It continues to deal with problems individually and separately, often at tremendous expense, and the result is that the total environment suffers, the quality of our lives continues to deteriorate.

The California Tomorrow Plan is actually two plans for two different Californias of the future. At the moment there are, of course, a number of possible futures for California but the plan identifies two prototypes, called "California One" and "California Two." It consists of five main sections:

**California Zero:** a summary of the major problems and disruptions which beset California today; a description of our traditional method of attempting to solve problems; and a sketch of an alternative way which shows considerable promise.

**California One:** a picture of the kind of California that will surely come to pass if the traditional California Zero way of solving problems continues into the future.

**California Two:** a proposal for the alternative way of solving problems; an outline of what government and private enterprise would have to do to carry out this alternative; a view of what life might be like in California Two.

**Comparisons of California One and California Two:** a general summary of the two Californias, with particular attention to comparative costs.

**Phasing in — California Two:** a list of specific actions which can be taken to bring California Two into being.

Finally, there is a chart showing some of the major provisions of the California Two plan.

We hold high ambitions for the state of California. To quote Barbara Ward, speaking a few years ago before a California Tomorrow conference: "First on the moon is fine; reaching out to the planets is splendid—I'm for it. But I think in the next 50 years, the first person who gives man a safe landfall in the city will be the man who makes the breakthrough to what the world really needs. I don't think it's too ambitious for California to choose the central preoccupation of man as its greatest challenge. . . . Any kind of working model would bring all mankind to your door."

This is a citizens' plan, an effort of individuals with very limited resources to show what a great state with its large resources could accomplish to preserve its beauty and enrich the lives of its citizens. Since the publication of a first sketch of the plan in March, 1971, California Tomorrow, assisted by other organizations, has held conferences and seminars throughout the state and in Washington, D.C., to discuss the plan (and the planning process) and to invite suggestions for change and improvement. Material received from these meetings and from innumerable other sources has inspired the preparation of this revised edition.

The plan nevertheless remains a sketch, a prefiguring of what might be, a beginning rather than a final statement and, again, a challenge, both to those who now wield power and to those who are critical of the "system": Are you making a better plan?

ALFRED HELLER

# California Zero

# California Zero

We are misusing our environment and ourselves to the point where amenities are rapidly disappearing, social order gives way to turmoil, and life itself is threatened. Our ways of doing things in California Zero, the California of today, need to be changed.

This California Zero section summarizes many of the problems which call for attention in California, and analyzes how we are now meeting problems and how we might meet them more effectively. It describes California Zero as a crossroad, and points to two main routes we can choose to follow from here.

Major disruptions that are besetting us in California Zero can be identified in two major categories—"Environmental resources misuse" and "Human resources misuse"—and in subcategories related to them.

The chart on page 10 summarizes California's "major disruptions" and forms the basis for much of the discussion that follows. On the following pages we describe many of the disruptions, under the three categories of Land, Structures, and People.

## Problems: Land, air, water

*Energy resources*

Most existing means of producing energy pollute or otherwise damage the environment. Some traditional fuel reserves are in danger of serious depletion or exhaustion. At the same time, the demand for energy is expected to double in the next decade.

Nuclear fission is now widely thought to be the answer to future energy needs, and utility companies plan to construct at least nine conventional nuclear power plants in the state by the year 2000. However, even with the construction of new generators, power shortages are likely in parts of California in the near future. The causes: population increase, industrial growth, and wasteful patterns of consumption. In order to meet this situation, new patterns of consumption will be required, for sufficient new sources of power are unlikely to be developed in the next decade.

Nuclear-fission plants entail the safe transportation and storage of dangerous, long-lived radioactive substances, and they may prove

## 21 Major disruptions

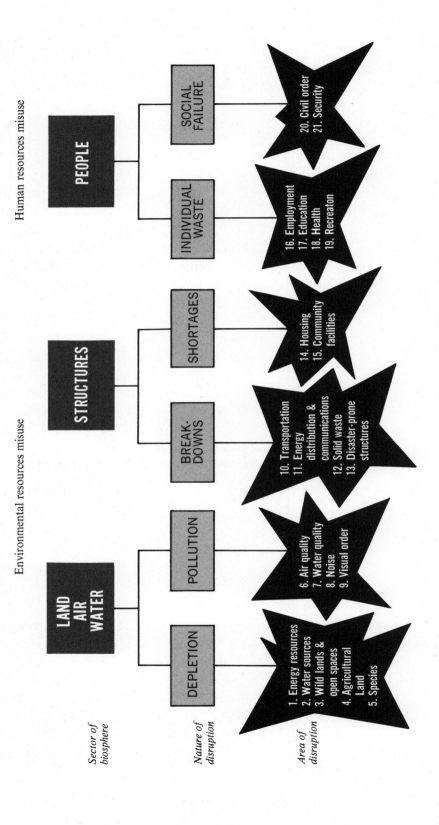

hazardous in earthquake zones. They will mar California's shorelines and may pollute its waters.

Safer and cleaner power sources that could be developed include California's considerable geothermal resources, and existing hydro-electric facilities equipped with reverse-pump generators for use during off-peak periods.

Long-range alternatives to present energy sources include atomic-fusion reactors and the harnessing of winds, tides, and solar energy.

All future energy policies and programs must effectively deal with the problem of waste heat, which otherwise may pollute our waters and produce undesirable climatic changes in our urban areas.

There now exists no state or national effort to develop a sensible energy policy with clear priorities for action, as part of comprehensive planning to serve human welfare and protect the natural environment.

*Water sources*

The California Water Plan, for which the current California Water Project is the first major step, provides Northern California water for future growth in Southern California and the San Joaquin Valley. Its authors assumed that such growth is wholly desirable and did not consider the impact on regions from which the water was to be withdrawn. Nor did they seriously consider possible alternatives to the transfer, such as limiting wasteful consumption, reusing treated waste water, and desalting ocean water.

Continued implementation of state water projects threatens to destroy our remaining wild rivers, along with their salmon and steelhead fisheries; worsen the pollution of San Francisco Bay; and heavily damage the Delta as an economic, recreational, and ecological resource.

Groundwater resources are endangered by excessive use and by contamination. Excessive use causes land subsidence, which reduces the land's water-storage capacity. Contamination makes existing water unusable.

*Wild lands and open spaces*

Much of California's wild land has been subjected to logging and mining activities, resort developments, and highway programs. The result—destruction of wildlife habitats and fisheries, loss of topsoil through erosion, stream pollution, and the loss of valuable open space and recreational land. For example, the State Department of Conservation recently reported that more than 500,000 acres of foothill land had been subdivided between 1960 and 1970. The report cited "significant environmental problems" as a result of such development.

Suburban development continues to devour large tracts of open land near our cities. Such lands need preservation; they beautify the urban environment, provide urgently needed recreational land for city residents, protect valuable watersheds, and increase the capacity of airsheds over smog-choked cities.

Two-thirds of all sea life is dependent on coastal estuaries. Two-thirds of California's estuaries have been destroyed by development. Of those that remain, another 42 percent are destined for destruction by the year 2000. Freeways planned for the coast will accelerate this process. They also will encourage the erosion of cliffs and beaches and stimulate extensive development along now-untouched scenic stretches of coastline.

The increased use of off-road vehicles—jeeps, snowmobiles, motorcycles—threatens the ecological integrity and disrupts the quiet beauty of the state's natural areas.

*Agricultural land*

California's agricultural productivity is enormous, one of the state's greatest resources. It is made possible by a combination of long growing seasons, rainless summers, and deep alluvial soils.

Yet each year, California loses 60,000 acre-feet of topsoil as a consequence of clear-cut logging, forest fires, cuts and fills from housing and road construction, and bad farming practices.

Extensive irrigation has caused a buildup of salts in the soils of the San Joaquin and Imperial valleys. As a result, millions of acres of productive land are threatened.

Originally, California had 8.7 million acres of prime agricultural land. Over two million acres of this land have already been urbanized. By 1980, almost one million additional acres will be subdivided, making a total loss of about one-third of our best agricultural land.

The continued subdivision of agricultural land results in the loss of a great food-producing resource, the disappearance of scenic urban greenbelts, and the loss of such "amenity" crops as avocados, artichokes, and lettuce.

The peripheral canal proposed for the California Water Plan could threaten thousands of acres of rich Delta farmland with damaging salt water intrusion and the San Francisco Bay with increased pollution.

Six species of native animals have become extinct in the state during the last 75 years. Forty more are classified by the State Depart-

*Species*      ment of Fish and Game as rare or endangered. These include the California condor, Santa Cruz long-toed salamander, brown pelican, desert pupfish, and bighorn sheep.

Over 500 species and varieties of California plants are classified as rare, endangered, or possibly extinct, by the California Native Plant Society. Among these are the San Francisco manzanita, single-flowered globe lily, and marsh paintbrush.

*Air quality*      All California communities with populations of 50,000 or more suffer from air pollution. In 1970, Los Angeles failed to meet federal and state air-quality standards for certain pollutants more than half the time. The San Francisco Bay Area failed to meet these standards more than one-third of the time. Rural areas up to 70 miles from major cities also have occasional smog.

Air pollution damages crops, timber, and livestock. California's annual agricultural loss from smog is estimated at $35 million. Equally important, smog degrades the human environment, is unpleasant and irritating, and is detrimental to human health.

Automobile exhaust is the major contributor to smog, yet state law does not explicitly give air-pollution control agencies the authority to limit automobile use during severe smog periods.

Although efforts are being made to reduce automobile emissions through exhaust-control devices, other approaches to solving this problem have been resisted or minimally supported by the "Freeway Establishment"—motor vehicle manufacturers, oil companies, trucking operators, auto clubs and others. These approaches include the development of rapid transit and of alternate types of engines.

*Water quality*      Water pollution in California is largely the result of improperly treated domestic sewage, industrial wastes, and agricultural run-off.

Water pollution destroys the habitat of aquatic life; spoils the aesthetic and recreational quality of lakes, rivers and bays; and presents a potentially serious hazard to human health.

Virtually all major rivers, bays, and estuaries are polluted, and pollution has destroyed many fisheries. Oil spills and oil-well blowouts have polluted our bays, beaches, and offshore waters, damaging property and wildlife.

Noise is a major ingredient of contemporary urban life, especially for those who can seldom escape the city. The noise from jet aircraft alone each day disturbs the peace of one million Californians.

*Noise,*
*visual order*

Visual order describes the harmonious relationship between man-made structures and their surroundings. Only rarely has this considera-tion influenced the course of development in California.

Freeways that destroy landscapes and divide cities, housing tracts that unnecessarily detract from the beauty of their settings, highrise buildings that cut off views, billboards that clutter country roads—these are some of the aesthetic problems that California has ignored.

## Problems: Structures

*Transportation*

Through gasoline taxes, the allocation of which is limited by the state constitution to highway uses, the public pays for new highways under a self-perpetuating system. Every year the state spends over $1 billion on its road systems and very little for other modes of transportation.

Heavy reliance on the automobile increases air pollution, destroys urban neighborhoods and rural open spaces, contributes to high noise levels, increases urban congestion, encourages urban sprawl, and costs local governments and taxpayers more money than would efficient alternate forms of transportation.

The poor and disadvantaged suffer most. Those who cannot af-ford to have automobiles are handicapped by the reliance of the majority on this single mode of transportation. Urban freeways often either destroy or isolate low-income neighborhoods.

Automobiles are dangerous. In 1970, California once again led the nation in the number of deaths and injuries from automobile ac-cidents. Deaths: 4,091; injuries: 241,589. To the extent they are avail-able, railroads and other forms of public transit provide relatively safer travel than do automobiles.

*Solid wastes*

Solid wastes produced in California every day average over 20 pounds per person, if one counts all wastes—municipal, industrial and agricultural.

Sanitary landfill is always destructive and often not sanitary. Valuable recreation land and wildlife habitats are destroyed by it. Nearby residents must endure both the unpleasant smell and the ugliness.

Municipal waste disposal is generally handled at the local level, but there is no organized system of management for most agricultural and many industrial wastes. The effects are polluted water, smells, ugliness, ecological disruption, threats to health, and reckless waste of natural resources.

*Disaster-prone lands and structures*

Fires and landslides are endemic in many areas of the state, yet zoning seldom takes this into account.

During periods of heavy rain, thousands of acres of California land are often flooded. The typical response to this problem is to build more dams and channel more streams. The result of this policy is a destruction of natural beauty and loss of wildlife habitat. Little consideration is ever given to floodplain zoning, which would provide open space, preserve wildlife, and protect human structures from damage.

Extensive building continues on land especially subject to earthquake damage—fault zones, unstable hillsides and filled areas. The February 1971 San Fernando earthquake is merely the most recent reminder of this constant threat. An earthquake of the magnitude of San Francisco's in 1906 could kill tens of thousands because buildings are situated along fault zones.

*Housing*

California is short of standard housing. We need over 500,000 new units today, as well as several thousand rehabilitated units. Present construction rates are well below the level necessary to meet this need.

Available conventional housing is too expensive for most buyers. Median income in the seven Southern California counties and the Bay Area counties (which together account for over 80 percent of California's population) would indicate a need for an average house price of about $19,000. The average price of a house in these counties is about $25,000.

More homes are being built for the $35,000-and-up market than for the under-$20,000 market. In urban areas of the state, almost 70 percent of the homes cost more than $18,000. Many people pay up to 35 percent of their incomes for housing that ill suits their needs.

The poor, concentrated in central cities and rural areas, have little chance to attain better housing. Urban renewal continues to reduce the supply of low-cost housing. Programs for housing farm workers require employer participation or the support of local government, neither of which is commonly available.

# Problems: People

*Employment*

During 1971, California's unemployment exceeded the national unemployment level. The average unemployment rate was seven percent which, translated into numbers, means that about 620,000 Californians were out of work at a given time.

The young and the ethnic minorities are hardest hit. Unemployment among black males aged 18 to 25 is two to four times higher than the average.

The aerospace industry, one of California's largest, is sensitive to economic fluctuations and changes in government policy. Because of government cutbacks, thousands of skilled engineers and technicians have been forced to search for jobs that no longer exist in the highly specialized fields in which they have been trained.

Retraining programs at all levels are very limited and highly ineffective. This is partly because of limited funds, but also because of the scarcity of new jobs and the existence of already well-qualified competitors for them.

*Education*

Signs of educational failure include an increasing high-school dropout rate and increasing functional illiteracy among California high-school graduates. The growing number of "alternative" schools also indicates dissatisfaction with California's educational system.

In colleges and universities, many students continue to see their schools as a training ground for an economic system that downgrades individual human aspirations, fouls the environment, and sustains foreign military adventures. The university continues to prepare students for some prestige professions that are no longer in demand.

Highly controversial issues such as busing, compensatory teaching, sex education and vocational training continue to plague primary and secondary education.

The State Supreme Court has ruled out the future use of property taxes as the basic means of financing public schools. As alternative solutions are devised, careful planning is required to insure that old inequities are not recast in new forms.

Vocational education in secondary schools, community colleges, and special schools is designed to provide marketable skills for young people and retrainees. It has had limited success because it does not reach many who might benefit. Many schools lack qualified vocational teachers and counselors and do not train potentially capable candidates for complex technical jobs.

*Health* — Health-care services in California are inadequate. Existing facilities are crowded, understaffed, and often located long distances from those they are intended to serve. Among the major health problems that persist in the state are malnutrition, alcoholism and drug abuse, venereal disease, dental disease, and frequent outbreaks of such contagious diseases as influenza and measles. All of these diseases could be controlled or eradicated by intensive programs of health education and preventive medicine and by the establishment of efficient, responsive community health centers.

Another major health-care problem is the enormous cost. The cost of living rose 25 percent from 1960 to 1970, but the cost of hospital care increased by 140 percent, and physicians' fees rose 45 percent. Today, even upper-middle-income families require health insurance to protect them from possible future medical expenses. Not to be insured can mean financial disaster.

Although we still have much to learn about the specific causal relationships between environment and health, we do know that air pollution, water pollution, and the extensive use of pesticides pose serious health problems.

Malnutrition of all kinds remains a serious problem in California despite the food-stamp and surplus-commodity programs. Many persons are underfed, but many more suffer the adverse effects of improper dietary habits.

There are about one million alcoholics in California. Less than five percent of these are now receiving treatment.

Estimates of the number of heroin addicts in the state range between 25 and 35 thousand. The trend is upward. In 1970, the number of adult arrests for heroin offenses was 10,900—up 11 percent from the previous year. Despite the failure of present policies to solve the narcotics problem, we persist in treating addicts as criminals rather than patients.

*Recreation* — Recreational facilities are inadequate in urban areas. Outlying park and wilderness areas are subject to overuse by urban populations.

In 1970, 16 million Californians lived within an hour's drive of the coast. By 1980, this figure will have increased to 20 million. Yet today, only 153 miles of the 1,067-mile coastline are open to public use.

Most recreational developments cater to middle-income families who can afford to own a boat, stay at a ski lodge, pay for overnight camping privileges, or own a summer home and a car to take them out of the city.

In many state parks, reservations for summer campsites must be made three months in advance. The number of days spent hiking and camping in California has more than doubled since 1955.

*Civil disorder*

Although civil disorder in the state has abated since 1969, the underlying causes have not. Many still see an unbridgeable gap between the rhetoric of politicians and the reality of any serious programs to end wars and improve the opportunities for a better life for everyone. The problems of unemployment, illness, educational failure, housing and transportation still are sources of anger and discontent. Failure to solve such problems may result in future disorders.

*Crime*

Crime has increased explosively in California and throughout the nation in recent years. During the last decade, the burglary rate in California increased by 97.7 percent; forcible rape by 105 percent; and willful homicide by 75 percent. The "law and order" issue remains sound political currency, but it can threaten civil liberties.

Our crime prevention programs are directed largely toward the symptoms of crime, rather than the causes. Putting more police officers on the streets, for example, will not reduce the number of heroin ad-

*Recurring themes*

The catalog of problems in California Zero is long. However, it shows certain recurring themes in each of the three problem areas of Land, Structures, and People.

**We are depleting our physical resources.** Prime agricultural soils, groundwater, fossil fuels, wildlife, and many other resources are suffering depletion, pollution, wastage, or destruction under the California Zero pattern of economic development. Pollution of air, land and water threatens not only amenities, but at times even life itself.

**The inadequacy of urban structures,** whether housing, transportation facilities or waste-disposal systems, reflects an urban pattern of

dicts who are forced to steal to support their habits.

Our correctional system reinforces criminal patterns, racial hatred and political discontent. The virulence of the problem is visible in the form of prison riots and hunger strikes and in a recidivism rate of approximately 45 percent among prisoners released from California state prisons.

## Dealing with problems: Two ways to go

Our traditional way of coping with problems has been to attack them separately, with little consideration of the relationships between one problem and another. Often this approach results in a worsening of the problems.

*An alternative to the traditional way*

Another way of coping with major problems is to seek out relationships among them, and then to identify some common, underlying causes. Policy is then directed at underlying causes instead of symptoms. The California Tomorrow Plan considers the potential effectiveness of both ways of coping with disruptions in the following two narratives of "CALIFORNIA ONE" and "CALIFORNIA TWO." CALIFORNIA ONE takes the traditional single-purpose approach to problems, often dealing with their symptoms rather than their causes. CALIFORNIA TWO looks to the causes and suggests more effective courses of action. (The chart on page 20 suggests the benefits, in one problem area, of dealing with the causes of problems instead of their obvious symptoms.)

---

life which has become increasingly congested, blighted, segregated, and difficult to govern, much less improve. And in the slurbs, the sprawling semicities of the metropolitan regions, many of the amenities of life are disappearing.

**Social problems persist despite present measures to solve them.** Patterns of employment are shifting and uncertain. There remain inequities in educational opportunity. People suffer from inadequate health care; society still requires that individuals take care of certain difficulties which in reality they are incapable of handling. A great many people feel that government is not responsive to their needs.

# Problems get worse unless responses deal with causes

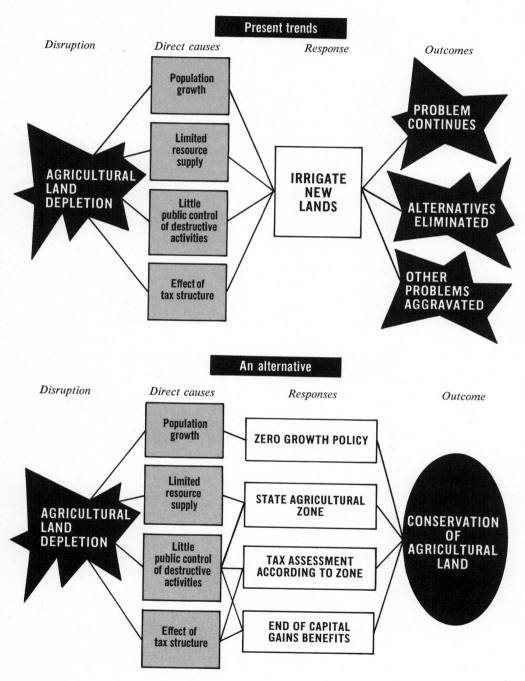

**Present trends**

| Disruption | Direct causes | Response | Outcomes |

AGRICULTURAL LAND DEPLETION

Population growth

Limited resource supply

Little public control of destructive activities

Effect of tax structure

IRRIGATE NEW LANDS

PROBLEM CONTINUES

ALTERNATIVES ELIMINATED

OTHER PROBLEMS AGGRAVATED

**An alternative**

| Disruption | Direct causes | Responses | Outcome |

AGRICULTURAL LAND DEPLETION

Population growth

Limited resource supply

Little public control of destructive activities

Effect of tax structure

ZERO GROWTH POLICY

STATE AGRICULTURAL ZONE

TAX ASSESSMENT ACCORDING TO ZONE

END OF CAPITAL GAINS BENEFITS

CONSERVATION OF AGRICULTURAL LAND

During the next five years, decisions will be made which will shape the growth and character of California to the turn of the century and beyond, regardless of whether the public participates in them or not. There are numerous choices available to us as we formulate goals, policies and programs for California in the years immediately ahead and fashion political and economic mechanisms to carry them out.

From a wide spectrum of possibilities we have outlined the two sets of choices. We have limited ourselves to only two views of the future, partially because of limited resources but also because comparisons can be made more clearly within this relatively simple format. Both CALIFORNIA ONE and CALIFORNIA TWO are set in the same time period —beginning in the early 1970s and ending at the turn of the century.

Regardless of what choices are made, there are certain exterior forces which we may assume will operate on any model of the future of the state. Some of our assumptions are as follows:

Despite a rapidly intensifying awareness of the dangers of unabated population growth, the worldwide population explosion will not diminish significantly within the next 30 years. Food and energy scarcities will create serious dislocations internationally, and to some degree within this country as well. By the year 1999, the population of California will have increased by at least ten million over the 1970 population of 20 million. This increase will happen even if the state effects a zero-growth policy in the 1970s, because of the large number of women of child-bearing age now in the population.

The economy of the United States will remain essentially "mixed," though government may assume greater or lesser responsibility for economic planning and control.

The basic republican structure of the nation, namely a federation of states under the Constitution, will remain intact. However, new forms of government will emerge at lower levels.

Despite present concerns about the destructive aspects of technology, our society will remain very heavily dependent upon technological development.

As machines take over more and more of the work formerly performed by men, society will adopt some new "post-industrial" values. Personal income will not be so closely linked to personal productivity. Leisure activities and avocational pursuits will tend to assume an importance approaching that of the traditional career jobs. Education will become an even larger concern than it is today.

New ideas may bring profound changes in our institutions and our actions, but self-interest will continue to be a basic source of individual motivation.

Finally, we assume that during the next quarter century mankind will be able to spare itself annihilation.

* * *

*California Two is preferable*

The next section of the plan describes CALIFORNIA ONE, and the following section CALIFORNIA TWO. For each alternative, we describe central, driving policies, important aspects of political and economic structure, and typical policies and programs designed to meet the major problems of the state. There are estimates of what life will be like in each California.

CALIFORNIA TWO is not intended as a formula for perfection, nor is CALIFORNIA ONE without advantages. They are offered, however, as real alternative approaches to the future. Although they are not the only alternatives available, they illustrate how sets of choices, made now, can bring about different lives for ourselves and our children.

In order to discount our prejudices, we have been cautious in our projections. CALIFORNIA TWO, nevertheless, seems to emerge as an eminently preferable alternative and, as such, constitutes the heart of the plan.

# California One

# California One

CALIFORNIA ONE is the kind of California that will surely come to pass if present methods of problem solving and policy making are continued. It is tomorrow's reflection of today's goals. It is the logical future consequence of California Zero.

## The absence of central policies

In CALIFORNIA ONE, problems of social and environmental disruption are still met—if at all—on an individual basis as they become visible and as the public becomes alarmed about them. Politicians pay lip service to "coordination" and "comprehensive planning," **but no integrated framework exists for making public policy.** Furthermore, there are no central, clearly stated, duly adopted public policies or goals; there is no shared vision of what California could become. Private organizations and government agencies continue to establish their own policies, whether or not they conflict with the general public interest. Frequently, programs conflict directly with each other, and the impact of one on another is ignored.

In CALIFORNIA ONE, some of the institutions and policies of California Zero have changed; but the general pattern of decision-making is the same. The quality of life in both our cities and countryside continues to deteriorate as problems outrace our attempts to solve them.

## How government works

The structure of state and local government in CALIFORNIA ONE remains essentially as in the early 1970s. The pattern of jurisdictional overlap, of agencies working at cross-purposes without any explicit system of priorities, continues in spite of the efforts of succeeding governors to group related functions into major agencies. Government grows enormously as new bureaucracies are added by the legislature in response to emerging problems.

Single-purpose action agencies and the special-interest groups who do business with them dominate the planning, budgeting and programming of the state government. Prominent among these are the Transportation Agency and the Department of Water Resources. These action agencies use population growth forecasts of the Department of Finance, as well as their own projections of traffic generation and water needs, to plan highways, a very few transitways, and massive aqueducts, unrelated to any comprehensive state conservation and development policy. All such single-purpose planning simply means that more complicated and intractable problems will continue to develop in the future.

Coordination among the agencies of government consists mainly of resolving major disagreements through *ad hoc* policy compromises.

The state Office of Planning and Research, established by the legislature in 1970, issues regular reports on the need for new programs of environmental conservation and new methods of coordinating the actions of state and local governments and the private sector to protect California's environmental quality. The effectiveness of the Office of Planning and Research is diminished, however, by a proliferation of other agencies set up to handle specific, critical environmental problems.

State regulatory commissions are set up to protect specially threatened areas or resources. For example, special commissions protect the coastline, mountain areas, the bays, and the desert. Some of these agencies lack authority or funds to implement programs or adequately police their jurisdictions. Others are captured by the groups they were created to regulate.

The governor's budget, prepared by the Department of Finance, is submitted annually to the legislature. The budgeting system employed tends to encourage uncoordinated, single-agency planning and programming. Each affected agency appeals to its own "establishment," which in turn brings effective pressure to bear on the governor and his staff.

Regional government is characterized by proliferating single-purpose agencies. Tentative moves toward unified administration are ineffectual. In all major metropolitan regions there are ever-growing numbers of separate, single-purpose bureaucracies with major regional responsibilities, such as air quality, waste disposal, open space, parks, transportation, water quality, shoreline protection, housing and ports. The boards making policy in these bureaucracies are often appointive and immune to effective citizen control.

Voluntary associations, largely representing local governments, are doing a good deal of regional planning, but they are slow to support anything except voluntary local compliance with comprehensive regional plans. These associations were originally created in the early 1960s to forestall genuine regional planning and administration, and in CALIFORNIA ONE they continue to do just that.

Cities, counties and special districts maintain the power to make major land-use and development decisions, including those affecting housing development. Private developers subvert and bypass local ordinances and standards by gaining variances and zone changes from pliable local officials.

Elections at all levels are dominated by large contributors, and this pattern results in overwhelming political power for major economic interest groups. The individual is often hard put to distinguish between the public and private sectors.

*The use of taxes*

Tax revenues in CALIFORNIA ONE are allocated primarily to physical development projects (highways, water projects, school construction) without reference to state conservation and development goals.

With few exceptions, taxes do not serve as positive instruments of policy. Many state as well as federal loan and grant programs to local governments and individuals are not closely tied to environmental quality considerations.

Tax policies of CALIFORNIA ONE tend to encourage wasteful patterns of growth. Tax advantages available for capital gains on land, for example, result in carving up the landscape for speculative purposes. Local property-tax assessments based on the idea that the "highest and best use" is found in intense development continue to turn the state's most fertile open lands into tract housing and parking lots.

In general, the economic policies of CALIFORNIA ONE make heavy demands on the state's natural resources, as the following section demonstrates.

## Views of the future:
## How California One meets typical problems

*Energy*

Demands for electrical energy begin to exceed the state's generating capacity, despite the construction of new power facilities. Power rationing and blackouts are not uncommon in major urban areas. There is no systematic program for developing new patterns of energy consumption. The state and the public utilities concentrate on a crash program to develop alternate sources of electricity, and utility rates are increased to pay for new facilities.

Nuclear reactors of the conventional type provide increasing amounts of our electrical power up to the year 2000. They pollute the air much less than conventional, fossil-fuel power plants, but their hot-water discharges result in the thermal pollution of lakes, rivers and bays, where cooling machinery is not employed. In addition, once-wild stretches of coastline are now marred by nuclear reactors.

The storage of radioactive nuclear wastes becomes a major issue. Underground storage facilities are planned for various sections of the country, but in many cases, local residents strongly object, and demand that these wastes be kept somewhere else.

*Water*
The state continues to assume a responsibility to provide water to match or even to encourage "growth" and development. There is limited progress in recycling of waste water and desalinization of seawater, but the state concentrates on completing the California Water Project. The North Coast is obliged to furnish both water and storage, losing much good land in the process.

The peripheral canal is constructed without any solid guarantee of maintenance of minimum outflow through the Delta. The ecological values of the Delta and Suisun Marsh are destroyed. Farming in the region becomes marginal. San Francisco Bay pollution increases, especially in the summer months.

In the effort to control pollution, the state's water-quality administration denies sewer hookups to overburdened systems. Swimming and fishing are forbidden in many rivers, lakes and bays. Incidents of sickness resulting from contaminated water increase.

Stricter legal controls on oil spills are written, and cleanup technology is improved. But catastrophic spills continue because of the doubled volume of oil shipment and the use of enormous tankers.

*Agricultural land*
The state continues to allow tax benefits to owners of agricultural land who agree to keep their land in agricultural use. At the same time, major statewide public works programs, and fiscal and tax policies, continue to encourage the urbanization of farmlands.

Along with a population that has grown towards 35 million, cities have spread out and have joined together north and south, taking over

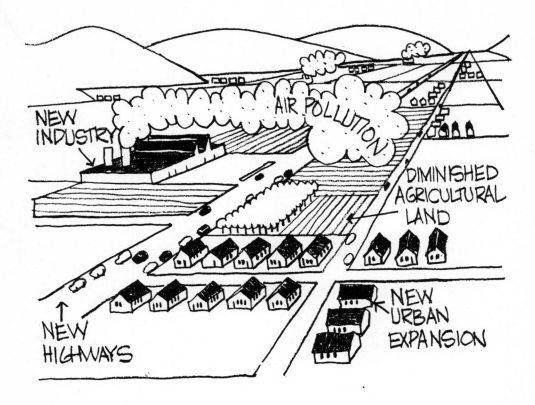

thousands of square miles of good land since 1970. The agricultural character of many regions disappears entirely.

New lands are irrigated to replace those lost to urbanization or ruined by extensive salt buildups, but these lands require expensive soil-conditioning treatments. The food they produce is of inferior quality. Food prices continue to rise.

*Wild lands and open spaces*

Commissions to protect open space and to provide some breathing space for people are established in large urban regions, but they cannot stop urban sprawl because they lack the funds and authority to set aside large tracts of threatened land.

State forest practices are improved; regulations and enforcement are strengthened. Flood-control projects such as large lined channels are developed in forest areas. Forest soil depletion and stream siltation continue, however, because regulations governing watershed management are inadequate.

Rivers, estuaries, and bays—and the life they support—are destroyed by siltation. Most of the state's remaining salt marshes and estuaries are lost to private development, power plants, and freeways.

Subdivisions of land in rural and mountain areas continue to cause erosion and stream pollution. Rural slums, some of them remnants of recreational subdivisions of years before, are spread across foothills, mountains and the coast. Wilderness established under federal regulations is endangered by increasing public use.

*Species* California's remaining salmon and steelhead fisheries are destroyed by the channelization, damming, and siltation of North Coast rivers. Fishing in or near urban areas drops off as a result of increased water pollution.

Species common in the early 1970s become scarce as their habitats are destroyed. Winter duck populations are especially affected. Many of the now-endangered species become extinct. Some rare species are protected in refuges and zoos.

*Air* Two components of CALIFORNIA ONE air-quality standards are motor vehicle exhaust-emission standards (established by the state legislature and met by emission-control devices) and pressure applied by regional air-quality control boards on industrial polluters, often forestalled by complaints of economic hardship. Alternatives to the internal-combustion engine, the chief source of air pollution, are steadily but slowly pursued by government and industry.

There is a slight drop in pollution levels in major metropolitan regions between 1970 and 1990. Then the improvement gained from reduced pollution per vehicle is lost because of the increase in the number of vehicles and inadequate controls over major stationary sources.

*Noise* Noise pollution increases with more cars, power appliances, etc. Allowances are granted residents and owners for soundproofing dwellings located under the approach cones of airports.

Limited-use zoning is enacted by some local governments in noise-afflicted areas adjacent to new airports and freeways, but effective legislation for control of noise is lacking.

*Transportation* Federal freeway funding continues at a high level. New funds become available for mass transit, special bus lanes, and shuttle buses. Major support of automotive transport, however, prevails well into the 1980s. Highway interests succeed in promoting an increase in gas taxes to meet freeway construction schedules.

Limited rapid-transit systems are built in Los Angeles, Sacramento, and San Diego. San Francisco expands the Bay Area Rapid Transit System. North-south passenger rail travel is improved with federal assistance.

People continue to rely on the automobile, despite increasing costs, air pollution, and congestion, because they are offered no incentives to do otherwise, and no real alternatives.

By 1999 there are 23 million automobiles in California. Traffic congestion increases even with additional freeways. Downtown centers have grown inaccessible as they have grown tall. They depend heavily on access by the automobile, but there is paralyzing local street congestion and parking is expensive and inadequate. Existing freeways have been widened or added to, up to quadruple decking. Inner-city populations still lack convenient access to many areas, both within and outside the cities.

Regional disposal districts are created to handle municipal wastes. Disposal is often by landfill in distant locations. Industries and farmers may or may not join, at their own option. City residents get the primary benefits of modern packaging; rural residents get most of the garbage that results.

Limited recycling of glass, paper, and metals such as aluminum and iron becomes an adjunct of the disposal process. Large-scale reuse by manufacturers requires subsidies, which are slow in coming. Little effort is made to separate organic and inorganic solid wastes, and to return organic wastes to the soil. No comprehensive programs of solid-waste disposal are developed that embody the principles of conserving resources and preserving the environment.

The packaging industry continues to produce nonreturnable, non-biodegradable containers, and litter increases despite a concentrated public education program by government, industry, and conservation organizations.

Natural disasters are still not rationally planned for. After each disaster, building and land-use policies continue along lines similar to those of the past.

Flooding is viewed as something to be controlled by engineering projects that channel and remove runoff. There is no policy of fire-area zoning analogous to floodplain zoning. Seismic dangers are acknowledged by adoption of statewide building-code standards. But there is no serious seismic zoning.

Fires continue to be an annual, late-summer trauma in Southern

California. New tract development continues along tinder-dry hillsides and canyons.

Eventually, another major earthquake strikes a densely populated urban area. Houses built along fault lines are severely damaged or destroyed. Buildings erected on bay fill collapse. Many highrise buildings sustain major damage despite assurances to the contrary. Hundreds, even thousands, of people are killed, injured, or displaced from their homes as a result of the earthquake. Property damage costs are estimated in the hundreds of millions of dollars.

*Housing*

To meet growing housing shortages, Cal-Vet loans, which aid three percent of the population, are continued, and there are loan funds for low-income housing developers.

Federal programs are reformed, revised, and consolidated. There continue to be rent supplements in one form or another; partnerships in urban renewal or model neighborhood projects; programs to find new construction techniques and new materials; reform of building codes.

Despite all federal and state, local and private efforts, however, California's housing needs are not successfully met. By 1990, millions of Californians live in unsanitary, crowded housing. Run-down core areas have expanded—accompanied by crime, drug problems, discontent, and a near-paralysis of public services.

Huge parks filled with mobile home-type dwellings cover the fringes of the metropolitan areas. The homes are close together, row

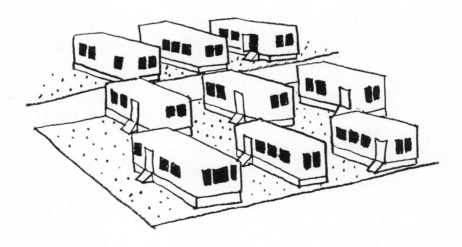

upon row. The parks deteriorate along with the dwelling units into new suburban slums that complement the growing urban ones.

There are not enough jobs, and there are inadequate income supports. Unemployment compensation continues to be the state's basic response to the continuing unemployment problem. State and federal retraining programs are started in many occupations, but because of heavy job competition the programs have limited success.

A national income floor alleviates survival problems for the poverty-stricken, and there are many other relief programs related to income—for example, aid to dependent children, rent supplements, food supplements.

Minorities still constitute most of the hard-core unemployed. Despite increasing union activity, farm laborers remain a large disadvantaged group in California. Small farmers displaced by urbanization and agribusiness are now competing for urban jobs. Many, with little experience in industry, join the growing welfare rolls.

The educational system seems largely irrelevant to the needs of society, unable to prepare people for vocation and avocation in a rapidly changing economy. Young people all go to school, but it doesn't help many of them find where they fit in. Schools continue to be isolated from the general political and cultural life of the community.

State policies regarding public health are directly connected to a national system of limited health insurance (superseding Medi-Cal and Medicare). Public health programs are relatively well planned, but the system only begins to meet the state's health needs.

Health costs continue to rise. The poor receive minimal health care, and individual ability to pay is still a determinant of the quality and frequency of the medical/dental care received. The need for medically trained personnel is acute.

Federal food-stamp and commodity programs continue, but many people, particularly in rural areas, are undernourished. Malnutrition remains a part of California life despite various state and federal programs.

Programs to deal with alcoholism, already under way, are continued and expanded. Alcoholics are no longer treated as criminals. Despite such programs, alcoholism increases as urban life grows more intolerable.

The state expands its program for rehabilitation of heroin addicts in state hospitals. Methadone clinics are established in many areas. The use of hard drugs remains a problem, however, and drug-related crime continues to be a serious problem in cities.

*Recreation*

Pressures on state and federal recreational areas are intense and destructive, in part because of a serious lack of adequate recreational lands and facilities at neighborhood and regional levels.

The state, counties and cities purchase and develop some areas of public value such as beaches, redwood groves and small open spaces in and near cities. But purchase programs do not include major threatened open-space areas, and residents in urban ghettos still have little opportunity to get to recreational areas.

*Crime and security*

Crime against persons and property continues to grow as a result of poor housing, unemployment and inadequate drug-treatment programs. The general response is agitation for more police and "stronger" laws.

In general, treatment of criminals continues to be punitive rather than rehabilitative. Recidivism rates remain high.

Police departments are manned disproportionately by whites, whose attitudes toward racial minorities and nonconforming youth frequently reinforce the general untrusting and hostile attitudes of these groups toward both the police and society in general.

An increasing number of crimes involves the use of guns, and the killing of victims, police and criminals. Efforts at gun-control legislation are repeatedly defeated.

Private security services expand, and closed-circuit television and other alarm devices are used increasingly by small businessmen and householders to prevent robberies. The threat of crime has grown to the point where nighttime foot traffic in major cities has almost ceased. Protective fortifications of various kinds surround many areas.

*Civil order*   The failure of CALIFORNIA ONE to solve problems of political and social inequities, or to meet urban and environmental problems, causes sporadic demonstrations and riots. The ghettos and campuses remain centers of unrest. Prison populations have grown and prison disruptions have become more virulent.

The public accepts harsh, repressive police measures, and preventive detention. New forms of reprisal on the part of dissenters, in the form of bombings, hijackings, and other disruption of public services (such as water supply and electric power) have emerged and increased as weapons of protest.

CALIFORNIA ONE is a tortured place. Sets of choices about the future still have to be made. But many possible alternatives, including CALIFORNIA TWO, now have been lost, perhaps irrevocably.

# California Two

# California Two

Right now, today, Californians could choose a more hopeful future than CALIFORNIA ONE. They could make a set of choices to maintain a thriving, beautiful state—CALIFORNIA TWO. This section offers an outline of how it might be done. It describes how underlying causes of disruption in the state can be identified in a systematic way, and basic or driving policies established to deal with the causes. It shows how driving policies developed in this way can form a sure framework for building a beautiful and productive California.

## The adoption of basic policies

How are basic or driving policies identified for CALIFORNIA TWO? First of all, the state establishes a State Planning Council (described in detail on page 43), and instructs it to develop these policies. The council does so after extensive public soundings, research and analysis.

*Finding the causes of disruption*

The procedure used requires the identification of underlying causes of disruptions in California. This can be done with the help of proven techniques of systems analysis. The chart on page 40 shows the results of a systematic probe. For each California Zero disruption listed across the top of the chart, there are a number of "direct causes," some of which are listed in the left-hand column. The matrix relating direct causes to disruptions demonstrates that certain causes or groups of causes recur.

The pattern which emerges shows four underlying causes of disruption:

*Four underlying causes*

**1. Lack of individual political strength** (arising from the structure and process of government).

**2. Lack of individual economic strength** (inadequate incomes, inequitable access to jobs, education, services, amenities).

# Four underlying causes of disruption emerge from the matrix of direct causes

**DISRUPTIONS**

| LAND/AIR/WATER | STRUCTURES | PEOPLE |
|---|---|---|

1. Energy resources
2. Water sources
3. Wild lands & open spaces
4. Agricultural land
5. Species
6. Air quality
7. Water quality
8. Noise
9. Visual order
10. Transportation
11. Energy distribution & communications
12. Solid waste
13. Disaster-prone structures
14. Housing
15. Community facilities
16. Employment
17. Education
18. Health
19. Recreation
20. Civil order
21. Security

**A PARTIAL LIST OF CAUSES**

A. Obsolete governmental institutions
B. Inaccessibility to effective individual control
C. Overcontrol of individual action
D. Distribution pattern of income, goods, and services
E. Effect of tax structure
F. Lack of finance
G. Little public control of destructive activities
H. Infrastructure location
I. Population growth
J. Consumption practices
K. Limited resource supply
L. Effect of market system

1 LACK OF INDIVIDUAL POLITICAL STRENGTH

2 LACK OF INDIVIDUAL ECONOMIC STRENGTH

3 DAMAGING DISTRIBUTION OF POPULATION

4 DAMAGING PATTERNS OF RESOURCE CONSUMPTION

● Major policies

**3. Damaging distribution of population** (both in numbers of people and in their location).

**4. Damaging patterns of resource consumption** (numbers of people, and the way they consume resources).

All disruptions seem to spring from one or more of these underlying causes. There are some overlaps; however, in general, causes 1 and 2 relate most often to our misuse of human resources and causes 3 and 4 relate most often to our misuse of environmental resources.

Once the underlying causes are identified, driving policies can then be designed to meet them, as follows:

Underlying Causes
of Disruption                                          Driving Policies

*Four
driving
policies*

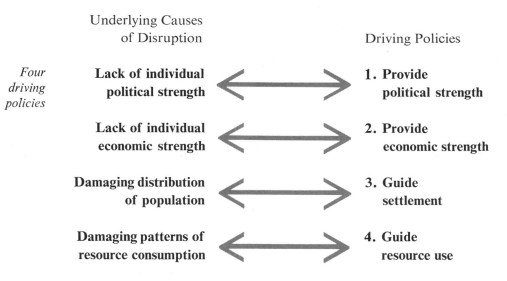

| Lack of individual political strength | 1. Provide political strength |
| Lack of individual economic strength | 2. Provide economic strength |
| Damaging distribution of population | 3. Guide settlement |
| Damaging patterns of resource consumption | 4. Guide resource use |

The four driving policies can be combined to express a single goal: "To provide for personal fulfillment within an amenable environment."

*Driving policies
and goal*

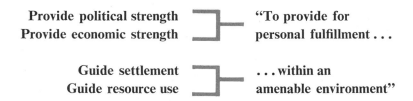

| Provide political strength | "To provide for |
| Provide economic strength | personal fulfillment . . . |
| Guide settlement | . . . within an |
| Guide resource use | amenable environment" |

Thus the State Planning Council identifies proposed driving policies for California. These are then submitted to the legislature for hearings and adoption. Once adopted, the policies form the basis for the organization and programs of government in CALIFORNIA TWO. They operate in all areas of concern, whether the issues involved are physical or social. They form a common framework for developing and coordinating all state programs and policies so that, for example, programs concerning energy resources, employment, and air quality support and sustain each other. The features of each of the four driving policies are described on the following pages.

# Driving Policy 1:
# Provide political strength

This policy provides the political framework for solving problems in California. It guarantees strong public control over state conservation and development policies at every level. It offers the opportunity for citizen involvement when policies and programs are being formulated, and when they are being carried out. This central policy is served through new or refurbished governmental institutions, and new rules of the game in the election process.

*State Planning Council*

Basic responsibility for both developing central policies for California, as noted above, and advancing them falls upon a State Planning Council.

The council consists of 11 members. Of these, the governor, who serves as chairman, and three members of his cabinet are ex-officio. The other seven members represent the general public. They are appointed by the governor and confirmed by the senate to serve four-year staggered terms.

Public members receive salaries equal to those of the highest-paid cabinet members.

Qualifications for public members on the planning council are established by the legislature. The council decides on its own organization and the work assignments of its members. It has its own staff. The members of the council are charged with serving the total, statewide interest. There is, however, an advisory committee to the council with representation from each regional government (page 46).

*Council responsibilities*

The council has the following responsibilities:

It prepares and annually updates a comprehensive plan, called the California State Plan, which specifies long-term and short-term state goals, policies, programs and budgets. The council absorbs the budgeting responsibility formerly vested in the State Department of Finance.

It works with the regions as they prepare regional conservation and development programs, and reviews them for the governor.

It also collects information and conducts hearings, studies and polls to meet its planning and budgeting responsibilities, and reports to the governor and the legislature on matters relating to state planning policy.

The council uses or has access to the most modern fact-gathering mechanisms available. With this machinery, the council is able to "test" the potential effects of governmental decisions which might be contained in the annual state plan/budget.

*The California
State Plan*

The California State Plan, prepared by the council, is the blueprint for achieving the goals of the state. Like this plan for CALIFORNIA Two, it is organized around the state's adopted driving policies. It contains:

**A section corresponding to Driving Policy 1**
(provide political strength), including
- plans for governmental organization and operation to increase the responsiveness and the problem-solving ability of government at all levels in the state;
- regulations concerning election to public office.

**A section corresponding to Driving Policy 2**
(provide economic strength), including
- plans to advance the economic interests of individuals;
- detailed specifications for the regional and state planning-financing processes.

**A section corresponding to Driving Policy 3**
(guide settlement), including
- a state zoning plan;
- a state infrastructure plan covering the location, design and construction of transportation, communication, water- and energy-distribution systems, and other public and private facilities;
- "California Standards" for environmental amenity to guide state, regional and local development and redevelopment.

**A section corresponding to Driving Policy 4**
(guide resource use), including
- a state population policy;
- state resource-use policies with recommended incentives and restraints;

**A budget section,** including
- a 10- to 20-year state capital-budget estimate in accordance with the plan;
- an annual state budget which consists of the next year's increment to the long-range plan.

*Executive and legislative responsibilities*

The governor receives annually from the State Planning Council the updated version of the California State Plan, including the budget. Guided by this, he submits to the legislature for adoption his own plan/budget. If his plan/budget is different from that prepared by the council, he must provide appropriate explanations of any modifications of the original version.

The legislature, in due course, adopts an annually updated version of the California State Plan, along with the coordinated state budget. In its budgetary studies, the legislature has full access to the computerized fact-gathering machinery used by the planning council. Following legislative action, the plan/budget is signed by the governor. After that, and until the next year's plan/budget is adopted, all legislative actions must be either consistent with the adopted plan/budget or framed as amendments to it.

The state's executive agencies have the responsibility of carrying out the provisions of the adopted California State Plan, in all programs and project proposals. Following the pattern of recent years, they are further streamlined into major functional areas. An environmental protection agency, for example, combines all of the state functions responsible for the natural environment, and becomes the major enforcement agency in this area.

In CALIFORNIA TWO, state regulatory agencies are reformed by legislation or constitutional amendment so that the state's driving policies and its adopted plan form the basis of the regulatory function.

*State planning: accountability to the public*

The structure of state government in CALIFORNIA TWO (combined with new regulations regarding campaign financing—described below) is designed to make the electoral process more democratic and closer to the people. State planning, programming and budgeting become fully visible for the first time, and the public can hold specific individuals —the governor or members of the legislature—more closely accountable than in the past for the direction of state government.

A reason for this is that all major state policies and expenditures are set forth in the comprehensive California State Plan, which is developed along clear lines of responsibility by the governor, the State Planning Council and the legislature. The council develops the annual plan/budget, but after he takes office, a new governor in effect takes control of the council. Holdover public members from the previous administration provide balance and continuity to the council, but the governor has final responsibility for presenting a plan/budget to the legislature.

The legislature, furthermore, must finally adopt a coordinated, systematically developed California State Plan and budget, as a unit. This provides a solid basis for judging legislative performance.

*Regional governments*

The political-economic structure of CALIFORNIA TWO is designed as a responsive, working system for solving problems, and essential to that system are multipurpose regional governments. In CALIFORNIA TWO, the legislature establishes governments for ten regions in the state (see map) and assigns them responsibility and authority for preparing and carrying out comprehensive regional plans.

Regions in CALIFORNIA TWO vary in size and degree of urbanization. They are established initially according to a map adopted in April, 1972, by the State Council on Intergovernmental Relations. The council's criteria in designating ten regional planning districts accepted the county as "the basic unit . . . No county is to be divided by a regional boundary." The criteria required that the regions conform to

physical and geographical makeup of counties including natural boundaries such as mountain ranges, valleys, drainage basins, bays, oceans, deserts and air basins;
communities of interest including common environmental problems, networks of transportation and transportation routes, common commercial and industrial interrelations, predominant living patterns in urban, suburban and rural areas, identification of residency and location of occupation, economic interdependency and existing political jurisdictions.

Each region has an elected legislative body, half of which is elected regionwide by a system of proportional representation. The other half is elected from individual districts within the region.

The regional executive branch is directed by the regional legislature. The executive branch is responsible for preparing the regional plan and budget, within the guidelines of the state plan and budget, and for implementing a regional conservation and development program, based on its plan.

# Regions of California

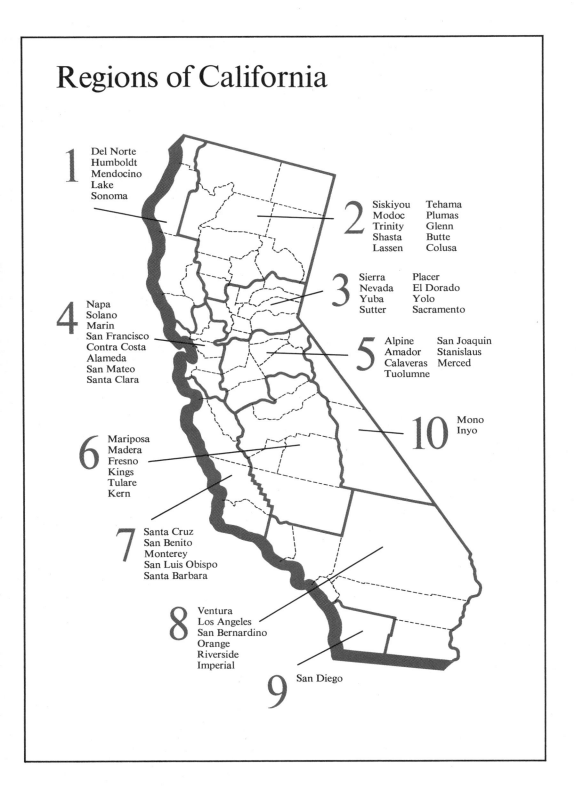

**1**
Del Norte
Humboldt
Mendocino
Lake
Sonoma

**2**
Siskiyou          Tehama
Modoc            Plumas
Trinity            Glenn
Shasta            Butte
Lassen            Colusa

**3**
Sierra            Placer
Nevada           El Dorado
Yuba              Yolo
Sutter            Sacramento

**4**
Napa
Solano
Marin
San Francisco
Contra Costa
Alameda
San Mateo
Santa Clara

**5**
Alpine            San Joaquin
Amador           Stanislaus
Calaveras        Merced
Tuolumne

**10**
Mono
Inyo

**6**
Mariposa
Madera
Fresno
Kings
Tulare
Kern

**7**
Santa Cruz
San Benito
Monterey
San Luis Obispo
Santa Barbara

**8**
Ventura
Los Angeles
San Bernardino
Orange
Riverside
Imperial

**9**
San Diego

The regional conservation and development plans and programs are concerned with human welfare. They are of quite another order from the popular concept of "land-use planning." They cover the full spectrum of social, economic and environmental concerns. They are intended to solve the major problems of the region, including those relating to employment, housing, education and health, transportation and recreation, as well as conservation.

Each regional conservation and development program is required to address itself directly to all major disruptions besetting the state, under the general categories of Land, Structures, and People (page 10).

The "Land" section of each regional plan, for example, provides for land, air and water conservation: open lands, parks, pollution control.

The "Structures" section covers urban development and redevelopment, including housing, transportation, waste treatment and other facilities.

The "People" section of the regional conservation and development plan and program deals with employment, education, health and social order.

As part of its planning responsibility, each region provides broad outlines for the plans and budgets of its local units of government, and in turn uses such plans and budgets in evolving its own comprehensive programs. It also assumes major responsibility for seeing that the activities of all governmental agencies in the region—federal and state as well as local—are coordinated to achieve regional goals as expressed in the regional plan and budget.

The region is the innovator. In preparing its conservation and development program, it works closely with federal agencies and local governments. It decides what existing state, local and federal programs it can use and what additional assistance it needs. The region must gain state and federal agency help, and move the entire planning-programming process along.

Any compilation of direct causes of the disruptions besetting California must find listings such as these (see chart, page 40):

"Little public control over destructive activities"

"Inaccessibility of destructive activities to effective individual control"

"Obsolete governmental institutions"

The regional governments of CALIFORNIA TWO are, in part, a response to the continuing inability of cities and counties on the one hand, and of the state or single-purpose districts on the other hand, to solve regional problems. The regions provide democratic control where it did not exist before, over regional issues such as housing, transportation, open space, waste disposal, and social welfare. The regional legislature, because it is elected partly by district and partly according to a proportional system, is broadly representative both of geographical areas and of differing viewpoints within the region.

Furthermore, the public has a new, strong voice to represent it as major policies affecting the region, such as those of the state infrastructure plan, come into being. The public was not always so well protected. For example, in the past, when the state highway commission decided upon major freeway locations, there was no authoritative regional voice, local interests were fragmented and without sufficient power to stand up to the state, and the most brutal excesses of the state freeway system resulted.

Regional government in CALIFORNIA TWO is, in addition, the vehicle by which the public not only devises practical, long-term solutions to major problems, but also gets the needed jobs done and paid for in a reasonable length of time. A description of the regional planning-budgeting-financing system of CALIFORNIA TWO is on pages 52 to 55.

*Cities and municipal counties*

The full responsibility for carrying out the regional program rests upon the regional government. But the regional government depends upon strong local governments which are fully involved in local planning and administration. Local government is strengthened in CALIFORNIA TWO.

Counties are established as municipalities. Consequently, there is no area of the state which is not under some form of municipal government, either city or county. City services and state and federal municipal aid are thus available to all urbanized areas.

*Community councils*

Citizen participation in city and county government is given new life with the creation of elected community councils. The geographic boundaries and specific forms of community councils, and the services they render, are determined by the city or municipal county in which they are located, in keeping with local needs. The East Palo Alto Municipal Council, established in 1967 by San Mateo County with the authorization of the state legislature, is one example of a community council.

In CALIFORNIA TWO, the cities and municipal counties are responsible for preparing local plans and coordinated budgets, under the guidelines of the state and regional plans. They administer local features of health, welfare, education, conservation and development programs. They have basic responsibility for local physical planning options under the state and regional plans. In carrying out their duties, the cities and counties may depend upon the community councils for assuming leadership in areas such as the following:

> the location and design of community facilities such as health centers, schools, employment information centers, and local offices of state, regional and municipal governments;
>
> the design and location of subunits of the regional or state transportation networks; the location and character of local parks and open spaces;
>
> the design and location of housing and other developments; and
>
> the provision of services related to all of these facilities.

The community councils in CALIFORNIA TWO also obtain municipal services for the public and bring public opinion to bear on all aspects of regional and municipal planning and administration.

The political structure of CALIFORNIA TWO is intended to afford the public stronger and more direct control over the shape and character of the state than it has ever had before.

*Election to public office*

A key element in this structure is a set of provisions which prevent elections from being dominated by special, powerful economic interests. These provisions include a tax credit for individual campaign contributions; strict laws requiring candidates to report campaign contributions, loans and guarantees well in advance of elections; a substantial shortening of time between primary and final elections; distribution of detailed information on all candidates in official voter pamphlets without cost to the candidate; the requirement that a specified amount of prime television time be made available to all officially qualified candidates, without cost; and postal and perhaps other subsidies.

# Driving Policy 2:
# Provide economic strength

This policy improves the economic well-being of individuals and enables society to pay for major social, conservation and development programs. It contains programs to stimulate the economy of the state and provide jobs and incomes for individuals. It also defines the procedures and provides for the financing by which entire regions can become desirable to live in, attractive, and flourishing. Driving Policy 2, with its emphasis on a strong economy, underwrites the achievement of the goals of CALIFORNIA TWO.

## Economic health for the state and its citizens

*Guaranteed minimum income*

In CALIFORNIA TWO, the maintenance of the economic health of the state and its citizens is a major concern of the state government. To provide a basic guarantee of economic sufficiency for everyone, state policy calls for and helps to obtain a federal program providing not a bare survival income, but enough for each family or individual to live in comfortable and healthful surroundings. An income floor is established, for example, at $6,000 a year (in 1972 values) for a family of four. It is tied to a work-incentive provision by which, up to a certain level, working people who earn more than the income floor can keep a portion of it.

*Economic advisory service*

The state's program for a strong economy includes an economic advisory service based on continuing, intensive reviews of the economies of the state and its regions. Thus the state provides guidelines for private and public decision-making with regard to economic development. It makes regular forecasts of economic trends, warns of vulnerable elements of the economy, offers suggestions on modernization, and points to gaps in services and industrial development. As part of its advisory service, the state assembles detailed information on the availability of jobs and operates a statewide computerized program to match job openings with individuals seeking jobs.

The economic advisories are closely coordinated through the State Planning Council with other state programs and policies. They recognize the need to protect and develop our agricultural and mineral resources in order to strengthen the economic base of the state. At the same time they recognize that most of the jobs in California, by far, are in service industries, and that these jobs are ultimately dependent on the maintenance of an attractive environment.

*State and*
*regional*
*building*
*programs*

State and regional building programs on a tremendous scale create many jobs, both directly and indirectly. These are long-term programs for meeting the state's economic and social needs. State projects could include the building of a new north-south, high-speed transit line along the western berm of the Central Valley, through the mountains to Los Angeles and San Diego, in keeping with the state infrastructure plan (page 59) and the state zoning plan (page 57).

Large regional improvement programs provide a major economic stimulus in CALIFORNIA TWO. They are comprehensive, multibillion-dollar conservation and development programs, dependent on heavy public and private investment, for housing, regional transportation, waste disposal, urban renewal, new-town construction and many other concerns. A description of how the regions plan, finance and carry out these programs is on pages 53 and 54.

*Jobs on*
*the land*

California works in particular to develop new jobs on the land. For example, agricultural cooperatives may be established in the state agricultural zone (page 57). The state accelerates efforts to provide new jobs, especially for youth, on federal and state lands in California. And instead of fighting the homestead concepts reflected in federal reclamation law, the state government supports the application of these concepts to open up new opportunities for thousands of family farmers on so-called "excess lands" of the federally irrigated valleys. The agricultural services of the University of California are reoriented, to help the family farmer as well as the large corporate operator.

## Paying for regional conservation and development

*A system of*
*planning*
*and financing*

In addition to serving individuals directly, Driving Policy 2—provide economic strength—includes a system of planning, budgeting and financing which translates an extremely broad range of popular goals into accomplishment. A key part of this system is a concept of financing for total regional conservation and development programs.

As noted under Driving Policy 1, for every part of the state in CALIFORNIA TWO, the state has established a strong regional government responsible for creating and carrying out a comprehensive, wide-ranging regional plan and program (see pages 46, 48).

*Federal Conservation and Development Bank*

Funding for the regional conservation and development program is obtained from state and federal sources, including publicly subscribed bond issues, and the resources of private capital, assisted by loan guarantees and other credit assistance from a Federal Conservation and Development Bank. Standards for private capital participation include a requirement that a fair share of the resources of lending institutions be allocated to social priorities.

In addition to guaranteeing loans, the federal bank, by action of the Congress, makes grants and long-term, low-interest loans to the regions. The loan repayments help to maintain, in effect, a revolving conservation and development fund.

Thus, in CALIFORNIA TWO, federal loans, grants and guarantees are applied to comprehensive regional programs covering physical development, conservation, and social concerns. In other words, federal funds are applied to help solve the state's major problems in a comprehensive and systematic way.

*Program development*

In brief, here is a step-by-step summary of how the regional programs are put together and paid for:

**First,** the regional plan identifies the particular problems of the region in each area of responsibility. For example, the plan examines the location, supply, and quality of housing in the region and identifies deficiencies.

**Second,** within state planning guidelines, the regional plan sets forth for each problem area a program to meet the deficiencies, using all resources available, private and public. In the case of housing, existing programs and procedures—involving, for example, FHA-guaranteed construction, ordinary privately financed housing, public housing, and various types of subsidized housing—would be applied to meet the identified needs, and coordinated with the overall financing provided by the Conservation and Development Bank.

**Third,** economic evaluations are conducted for each area of responsibility. The economic evaluation includes a benefit-cost study. This is a balance sheet which shows full costs of a program as against full benefits.

In addition to a benefit-cost study, the economic evaluation includes a study of financial feasibility which shows to what extent the program can pay for itself. This study lists and compares all expected public and private expenditure for the program and anticipated income in connection with it. Thus, a study might take into account federal and state grants and loans; income from sources such as the sale of services; taxes generated by the program; and the major and essential participation of the private sector.

**Fourth,** economic evaluations for all areas of responsibility are then combined, rationalized and totaled, to arrive at a comprehensive analysis for the total regional conservation and development program.

In other words, a total program is prepared to meet the major problems of a total region, and demonstrated on balance to be economically justified and feasible.

Traditionally, large public works have been financed through single-purpose federal grants (interstate highways, urban redevelopment), single-purpose bond issues (schools, rapid transit, water systems), or single-purpose loans (dams). Some public works, such as strategically placed bridges, are very profitable, while others, like public housing, operate at a loss. In CALIFORNIA TWO, the concept of comprehensive, low-interest financing is used to underwrite all aspects of regional development. Revenue-producing investments are included with nonrevenue-producing investments in one economic package.

By this procedure, for example, strong revenue-producing elements of the regional program, such as water development and distribution, can help carry drug rehabilitation programs.

**Fifth,** the regional government adopts its conservation and development program and accompanying financing proposals. These include yearly performance budgets in each area of responsibility, and a listing of projects by priority.

The total regional program, the analyses supporting it, and the financing arrangements are covered in a comprehensive authorizing document prepared by the region.

**Sixth,** the State Planning Council must certify that the program is within the guides of the California State Plan. The governor then submits the total program to the Congress and asks for authorization of the federally guaranteed and funded parts of the program. In other words, the Congress considers a full regional program, perhaps involving several billion dollars of public funds, before authorizing the federal features of it. This employs, on a large scale, procedures similar to those used in the past for area resource-development programs prepared by the Department of Agriculture.

After federal authorization, the regional program receives yearly funding through the budgets of the regional, state and federal agencies involved and from the Federal Conservation and Development Bank.

The regional government makes an annual report on the progress of the total program and recommends changes as necessary. Its conclusions are transmitted to the appropriate congressional committees and the federal agencies involved, and reflected in the annually adopted regional plan and budget and the budgets of local government.

* * *

Not only does regional government in CALIFORNIA TWO have the financial resources for achieving its program, it also has the necessary machinery at its disposal to meet its obligations.

*The region assesses property taxes*

For example, state assessment policy enables the regional government to assess all property taxes in the region. The region uses a portion of these monies for its own support, and allocates the remainder to the cities, municipal counties and other governmental agencies in the region on the basis of local needs reflected in the regional budget. This is a major tool to help the region coordinate the activities of other agencies, in carrying out its conservation and development program. It is a means for equalizing the tax burden within the region.

*Public corporations*

In order to help realize regional plans, the state authorizes regional governments to charter public corporations capable of carrying out large-scale, integrated regional projects from planning to land acquisition through construction and leasing. The New York State Urban Development Corporation, established in 1968, is an example of a public corporation.

An entirely new community might be built by a public corporation, as an example. The corporation operates by the rules of the state and regional plans. No housing is planned in zones subject to hazardous earthquakes, fires, floods, or landslides. State agricultural and conservation zones and amenity requirements are incorporated in project plans.

Aided by loan guarantees and by grants and loans from the Federal Conservation and Development Bank, the corporation plans the new community and buys the land, through eminent domain if necessary. It may construct and lease the facilities on its own or by contract. It can also lease land to other entities for housing and for commercial purposes. Surplus funds go to support underfinanced but necessary projects in the regional program. The corporation builds parks and schools, and transportation facilities to connect with the regional grid. It does what is necessary to complete its project in every aspect.

Regional renewal programs in established cities are carried out by public corporations in the same way.

## The federal role

It is not possible for any state to guarantee economic sufficiency without the strong support and cooperation of the federal government. California could on its own provide an income floor or establish a conservation and development bank, similar to those proposed for the federal government in this plan. But it is unlikely that the state could be persuaded to do so, even if it could muster the needed financial resources. Unless these benefits were made available to all states, California would fear that in acting independently it would defeat its own purpose by attracting more in-migrants than could be accommodated.

In CALIFORNIA TWO, the state helps persuade the federal government to take the needed action. As the most populous state, it can have tremendous influence on federal policy. Thus it is in good measure in response to California's leadership that the federal government creates the Federal Conservation and Development Bank and provides regular financing for it.

Furthermore, encouraged by the California model, the federal government requires all the states to apply for loans and other forms of assistance on the basis of comprehensive regional plans prepared by governments which will carry them out.

# Driving Policy 3: Guide settlement

This policy is aimed at eliminating damaging distribution of population in California by establishing a new framework for settlement. There are four main parts of this policy:

- a state zoning plan, which defines in general which areas may be built upon and which may not;
- a state infrastructure plan for California's public utility arterials (transportation, water, wastes, energy, information) upon which development depends;
- a set of "California Standards" having to do with environmental quality and amenity, and public facilities and services;
- a state policy on population (described under Driving Policy 4).

## State zoning plan

The state zoning plan serves both Driving Policy 3 (guide settlement) and Driving Policy 4 (guide resource use). It protects the state's most valuable open lands, including prime agricultural soils; effectively checks urban sprawl; and protects green space in metropolitan areas.

Under this plan, which is, of course, part of the adopted California State Plan, all the lands of the state are placed in one or another of four zones (see map). The precise boundaries of the zones, and restrictions on usage in each case, are set forth by the state primarily on the basis of thorough ecological and use-capacity surveys of the state's lands, but also with due regard for the land-use implications of state policies in all areas of concern. Thus the state zoning plan is one expression, through regulatory mapping, of how demands for urban expansion are to be reconciled with demands for the maintenance of environmental quality.

The four zones are:

*Four state zones*

**Agricultural:** Lands with a high capacity for intensive cultivation are included in this zone. Maximum building density on these lands is one unit per 25 acres. Provision is made, however, for the establishment of small agricultural communities (see page 52). This zone is ad-

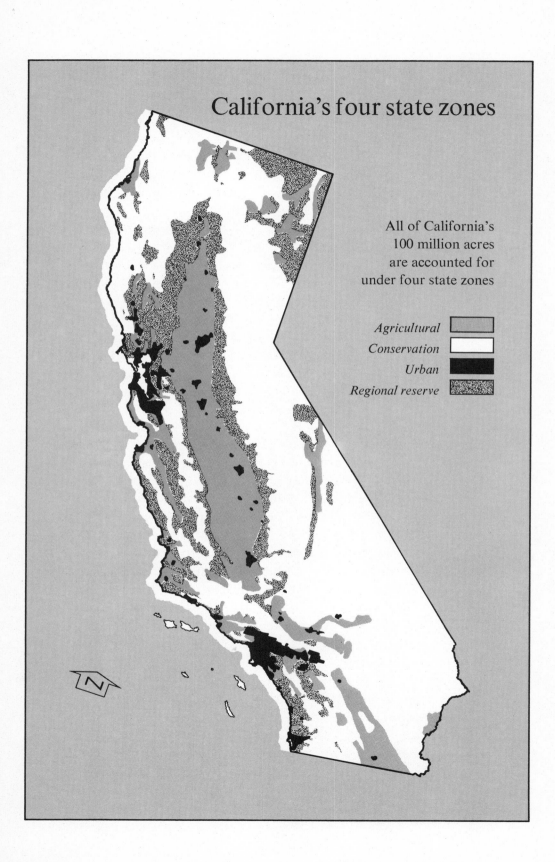

# California's four state zones

All of California's
100 million acres
are accounted for
under four state zones

*Agricultural*
*Conservation*
*Urban*
*Regional reserve*

ministered by the state through its environmental protection agency.

**Conservation:** The conservation zone includes lands for protection of ecologic, scenic, historic, and archeologic values; the preserves of threatened or unique animal or plant species; lands for conservation of water, forest, rangeland and desert resources, and game; open water, shoreline and aquifer-recharge zones; and fire, flood, erosion, or earthquake hazard areas. Some resources in this zone, such as timber, are available for controlled production.

In the conservation zone, lands are classified as nonbuildable, or conditionally buildable under strict controls which protect the specific qualities of the land which the zone is established to safeguard. Conservation lands are state administered and protected mainly under the police power, but also by outright purchase or less-than-fee purchase of development rights.

**Urban:** This zone includes lands which do not fall in either of the first two categories and which have already been urbanized. Lands in this zone are administered by the regional governments, according to state standards and their own respective regional plans.

**Regional reserve:** Lands which do not fall within any of the first three categories are set aside as regional reserve, a "general use-conservation" category. They may possess some positive value for controlled future development and other uses, in addition to conservation. They are administered by the regional governments and are a key to flexibility and variety in regional development. Within the standards and requirements of the California State Plan, the regions may plan to keep these lands largely as open space, or use them for a variety of public and private purposes.

## State infrastructure plan

The infrastructure is the backbone of development in California. It includes airways, railroads, freeways, power plants, transmission lines, dams, aqueducts, bridges, bicycle ways, transit systems, streets and highways, seaports, and airports.

The state infrastructure plan locates sites and corridors for these components based on determinations about the state's economic future and patterns of employment, within the broad context of the

California State Plan, including the state zoning plan. There are detailed design standards for all parts of the infrastructure which are interstate or interregional in nature, such as trunk freeways or a new north-south, high-speed rail line. The infrastructure plan outlines federal and state responsibilities for the financing and construction of these components. There is a listing of construction priorities, and a timetable.

A well-considered plan of this kind cannot be carried out under unduly restrictive financing arrangements. The state therefore works to end federal and state programs such as those which have directed transportation funds exclusively to highway programs.

The infrastructure plan also includes general design requirements for the infrastructure parts which are intraregional in nature, but the planning and construction timetables of major regional public works, such as intraregional transit, are the responsibility of each region in its conservation and development program, within the guides of the California State Plan.

## California Standards

The California Standards are statewide minimum requirements for environmental quality and amenity, and for public facilities and services. They are based on the principle that "amenity"—the pleasantness and attractiveness of our environment—is an essential concern of public policy; mere survival is not enough. They govern programs of state, regional, and local government, and the private sector.

Following are examples of California Standards:

*Maintaining environmental standards* ━━━━━━━━━━━━━━━━━━━━━━━━

The capacity of air and water to assimilate wastes is a resource that belongs to the people. But it is a limited resource. In CALIFORNIA TWO, use of this limited assimilative capacity is a privilege that is not only regulated but paid for. Abuse of the privilege is penalized.

Hence, if waste dischargers release wastes to air or water within regulated limits, they are charged a fee proportional to the amount of waste discharged, not only as a matter of equity but also as an incen-

**Air quality.** The regions of the state must maintain a level of air quality that fully protects health, provides amenity (i.e., clean air), is harmless to all forms of vegetation, and does no damage to property. This is defined by ambient air standards adopted by the state (statewide and by air basin).

Emission standards are based upon computations of the specific carrying capacity of the regional air basin in question, in terms of the size and diffusion pattern of the air mass at times of thermal inversion.

A typical regional plan achieves air-quality standards not only by regulating emissions from each type of source, but also by controlling the number and location of the sources themselves (such as industries, freeways, power plants, commercial establishments and homes). It controls emissions from moving vehicles by establishing and enforcing emission standards, by bringing into being nonpolluting forms of public and private transportation, and by restricting the number and use of individual vehicles.

**Water quality.** The water-quality standards represent a commitment to high water quality for all state waters, fresh or salt. The standards are intended to insure a good environment for people, and to protect ecosystems, not merely to protect public health. They keep the waters of California clean and clear.

They require that wherever wastes are discharged into waters, fresh or salt, surface or underground, the wastes themselves must meet the standards set for such waters. This is necessary because we are very close to the time when the total volume of liquid wastes equals the total volume of runoff.

Surface waters in the conservation zone and the undeveloped por-

---

tive toward zero emissions.

If waste dischargers violate the regulations, then in addition to the fees referred to above, they are subjected to fines ranging from $10,000 to $100,000 per day.

Strong enforcement by the state environmental protection agency of these and other regulations pertaining to environmental quality is an essential component of the CALIFORNIA TWO model.

tions of the regional-reserve zone are kept in as near a natural state of quality as possible. No waste discharges whatsoever are permitted into mountain streams or alpine lakes.

In agricultural, urban and developed regional-reserve areas, waste waters percolated into the ground or discharged into surface waters cannot contain toxic substances in excess of drinking-water standards. Nitrogen content of waste waters is controlled so as to prevent health hazards from groundwaters put to domestic use, and to prevent the possibility of algae blooms in surface waters.

In basins known to have an adverse salt balance, the salt content of waste waters discharged on land may not exceed that which would result from normal domestic use of the original water.

The minimum standard for surface waters in state agricultural and urban zones and in developed portions of regional-reserve land may be expected to become progressively more strict with time.

**Pesticides.** No chemical poisons of any kind may be marketed until the manufacturer has demonstrated that the short- and long-range effects of their use will not damage the environment of the state. The final judge is the state environmental protection agency, working through the state health authorities.

**Open spaces.** Minimum open-space standards for recreational lands are established for the regions. The basic state standard is 20 acres of regional parks per 1,000 population within 40 miles of population centers.

In addition, ten acres of distributed green space per 1,000 people in a given community are required. At least half of this must be unpaved public park land at ground level.

**Noise.** This standard is a commitment to keep noise at levels not merely tolerable but consistent with good health and comfort. Maximum outdoor sound levels are established by the State Department of Public Health and related to the time of day, the environment involved, and the source of the noise.

A typical regional plan helps to insure regionwide adherence to the outdoor sound standards by controlling the distance between noise sources and places of residence, recreation, schools, etc. It establishes buffer areas, for example, adjacent to freeways and airports.

**Housing.** The state declares and assumes its responsibility for assuring decent housing for all the people of the state. Regional plans and development programs are required to conform to this policy. Regional housing plans must provide for sufficient housing to serve the people of all income groups, assuming that no more than one-fourth of an individual's income will be applied to housing; they must show a distribution of housing which enables any person to live in the area where he works and enjoy the environmental and social amenities of that area.

Minimum amenity requirements for housing are developed—relating, for example, to the availability of sunshine or privacy—to complement the more conventional statewide construction standards dealing with basic health and safety.

**Access.** Maximum time periods are set for travel between any residence and certain essential community facilities in urban areas. For example, ten minutes by foot to a local park; 15 minutes by public transit to a health-care facility and elementary and secondary schools; 25 minutes to a central business district.

**Public facilities and services.** For urban public facilities and services, there are quality standards which the regions must meet in their plans and development programs. Where necessary, the state carries on programs to help the regions in doing so. The standards are based on the principle that every citizen must have safety, the opportunity for education and good health care, and a range of work choices within his community. The standards include requirements for:

- Regional and community health-care facilities, which provide all Californians easy access to all needed health services. (See pages 73 and 74 for a summary of state health standards, and a typical regional health-care program.)
- Educational, recreational and cultural facilities and programs, designed to develop the role of schools as centers of community cultural affairs for all ages.
- Employment centers, to function as clearing houses for employment information. The centers are linked by computer to a statewide network, established under the state infrastructure plan.
- Conveniently available public facilities and services, such as

government offices, courts, jails, fire and police protection and solid-waste removal or recycling.

- Correctional facilities, emphasizing rehabilitation of criminal offenders (including community units using successful techniques such as those developed by Synanon).

- Community centers, which combine many of the foregoing facilities and services, must be considered in regional plans for urban development. In addition to the economies they may offer, community centers can have the effect of coordinating separate programs. For example, the full integration of employment information centers with educational-cultural facilities could generate training and retraining programs, or the teaching of crafts and skills appropriate to the needs of the community and the state.

# Driving Policy 4:
# Guide resource use

Wasteful and damaging patterns of resource consumption constitute an underlying cause of California's environmental problems (see summary, page 41). Driving Policy 4 is designed to conserve the state's great resource base, not just for this year, but for a thousand years, by establishing new patterns of consumption. It is the means by which Californians can manage land, air, and water resources as essential parts of the life-support system upon which everyone depends.

Some portions of Driving Policy 3 (guide settlement) directly serve the purposes of Driving Policy 4. For example, the state zoning plan helps protect all of the lands of California from further urban sprawl. And as air- and water-quality standards are followed, consumption patterns change.

In addition, Driving Policy 4 is served by a state population policy to limit the number of consumers, and programs to guide resource use and limit what people consume. Driving Policy 4 ends the profligate use of resources and encourages recycling. Like the others, it depends on federal as well as state action.

## State population policy

*Zero population growth: a first step*

Increasing population has been identified as a contributing cause of almost every environmental and social problem in the state, as well as in the nation and the world (see chart, page 40). In CALIFORNIA TWO the state aims for a stable population, to be achieved as soon as possible without the use of unacceptable public controls. The legislature and the governor also urge the federal government to adopt a similar policy, and programs to back it up.

A zero population growth policy adopted for California before 1975 results in a leveling off of the state's population at 30 million by 1999.

A population level of 30 million is not a goal. It is merely the result of a prudent first step toward placing some rational limits on the number of people who can live amenably on the land of California.

The optimum stable population for California may be determined to be considerably lower.

*Action across a broad front*

To achieve its population goals the state takes firm action in several areas. For example, it adopts financial incentives, such as limiting income-tax exemptions to two children. Through its health program, it guarantees the availability at low cost of the full range of birth-control material and services and widespread dissemination of birth-control information.

In addition, the state urges the federal government to use equitable and constitutional means to keep in-migration from putting undue strain on the institutions and amenities of the states. A national policy on settlement, carefully developed and consistently applied, could begin to direct economic activity and jobs to areas capable of absorbing additional environmental impact. Federal assistance programs such as the income minimum proposed in Driving Policy 2 also help to raise and equalize social benefits among the states, thus reducing the special attractions of progressive states such as California.

The State Planning Council, working with the regions, conducts research into optimum population levels—how many people can live in reconstructed settlements and how many should be planned for in new ones—as part of a continuing process of testing and refining the state's population policy.

## Programs to guide resource use

Many of the programs of CALIFORNIA TWO to discourage wasteful use of resources seem drastic and will have considerable effect upon the economy of the state. However, the state's environmental carrying capacity is the measurement for not only the number of people in California, but also the level of per-capita consumption of natural resources. Neither can be allowed to run free.

Following are examples of programs to guide resource use. Economic incentives as well as regulations are used to help eliminate damaging patterns of consumption.

*Energy resources*

The state plays a strong role in ending the serious depletion of traditional energy resources and developing new, pollution-free energy such as geothermal power. It formulates a **program of energy usage** according to realistic appraisals of immediate and long-term requirements and supplies.

To discourage undue depletion of existing energy resources, for example, the state levies a **tax on consumption of electricity** by individual consumers. Average consumption levels are set, varying with the time of year and size of household. Above these levels, taxes are levied in a graduated manner. In addition, the legislature requests Congress to establish a federal tax on large-scale industrial consumption of energy resources.

**State building requirements** encourage the siting of buildings to take advantage of solar heat; the elimination of unnecessary systems such as air conditioning when natural methods such as cross ventilation are adequate; the reducing of light levels and the use of natural lighting wherever possible; and an end to the excessive use of glass and curtain walls with reliance on air conditioning and heating to compensate.

To conserve disappearing oil reserves, the state substitutes an **oil depletion tax** for the oil depletion allowance, and calls for a similar federal tax policy. The cost is passed on to users, which encourages lower consumption of this resource, less pollution, and the development of alternative energy sources.

A graduated tax is placed on **automobiles exceeding 65 h.p.** to encourage the use of small automobiles. Small cars require less raw material in their manufacture, consume less fuel, and demand less space on roads and parking lots than former standard-size vehicles.

*Protection for the land*

To protect open land from speculative pressures for development and encourage appropriate development in urban areas, **land is taxed according to its zoning category,** and not according to its potential for development.

Assessments on land in each zone are made on the basis of optimum, not maximum, use. Thus agricultural parcels, to take one example, are taxed on the basis of what the land can yield under good agricultural practices. If a given piece of land can produce four tons of hay per acre, taxes under this principle do not force the farmer to raise six tons per acre by the use of chemical fertilizers.

Buyers of raw land are no longer able to take the **capital gains benefit** on their profits when they sell. This outdated provision in state and federal tax law encouraged the most destructive kind of land speculation and development. It is eliminated in CALIFORNIA TWO by a change in state income-tax law and a similar change in the federal law, brought about through the aggressive initiative of the governor and the legislature.

The state protects a variety of minerals and raw materials from harmful depletion. For example, there is a tax on building materials, such as redwood, which represent limited resources.

*Water use*     The wasteful use of California's water resources is ended. Inter-basin water transfers are no longer permitted simply to sustain population growth or increased consumption in water-short areas. Any inter-regional exchange is contingent on programs of desalinization, total reclamation, and recycling. The total costs of developing and transporting water are charged to its users.

*Recycling*     The practice of recycling—of using resources over and over again —becomes an important part of the process of living in California. It is encouraged in ways such as the following:

There is a **tax on containers and packaging materials**—cans, bottles, plastics, cardboard and paper. Receipts from such a tax help to promote regional solid-waste disposal systems. To encourage recycling, the government establishes price supports so that salvaged wastes are sold back to industry at competitive prices. At the same time, the state sponsors research into efficient, economical recycling processes.

There is a special **tax on automobiles** sufficient to pay the costs of their eventual recycling.

The state of California discourages the building of new structures when old ones can do a satisfactory job. Changes in policy make **reuse and multiple use of existing structures**—houses, buildings, rights of way—increasingly appealing. Regional plans are required to contain surveys of existing structures, by type, with inventories of structures currently in use, of those vacated or capable of rehabilitation, and of those which offer a multiuse potential. The regional development programs must give preference to areas and buildings available for upgrading, especially those designated by community councils.

Regional and community transportation plans must emphasize more intensive use of existing rights-of-way, and ways to cut down on urban travel (meetings via closed-circuit television, for example).

The damaging patterns of consumption which have hurt California so badly in the past occurred because the public allowed them

*Education
for a
"land ethic"*

to. A "land ethic" was something that might be needed somewhere else, in places less abundantly endowed. In CALIFORNIA TWO, programs of education convey the importance of adapting the California life-style to the reality of limited resources.

For example, the state educational curricula on the environment emphasize comprehensive resource management and its relationship to the state's resource-conservation goals. Course curricula in the teaching of general ecology are laid out to include both theory and practical experience on the land.

# Views of the future:
# California Two in operation

The four driving policies are intended to work together to solve the state's major problems. Will they? How can the CALIFORNIA TWO framework be applied to critical problems? One way of finding answers to these questions is to take recognized problems and "test out" how well CALIFORNIA TWO, with its emphasis on regional planning and development, would deal with them. Following are three examples of this process.

## Three case studies

### 1. How can needed open space be assured in Santa Clara County?

In the 1960s and into the 1970s, the lands of Santa Clara County were urbanizing at the average rate of nearly 4,000 acres per year. Most of this development took place on the prime agricultural land of the Santa Clara Valley.

*Open space in Santa Clara County*

In CALIFORNIA TWO the zoning action of the state, along with the reformed system of land taxation, stops uncontrolled development of agricultural and other open-space lands. This affects Santa Clara County as follows:

All lands in the south Santa Clara Valley which are not presently urbanized are zoned "agricultural." Remaining prime agricultural lands in the north valley are also zoned agricultural (except for single or contiguous units which together do not exceed 25 acres in size).

Forested land and watersheds in the Santa Cruz Mountains, steep slopes in the Mt. Hamilton range, and bay lands and marshes are zoned "conservation."

Lands of the Santa Clara Valley already urbanized are zoned "urban."

The eastern foothills and plots of open land under 25 acres within urban areas are zoned "regional reserve."

Because open land in CALIFORNIA TWO is zoned by the state, and only the state can change the agricultural and conservation zones, the land is protected from pressures for development. Speculators are discouraged from buying open lands in the hope of converting them to urban uses. Because all lands are assessed for tax purposes according to their zones, owners of agricultural and other open-space lands are no longer forced to sell out under tax pressures.

The government of Region 4, which includes seven Bay Area counties, is required by law to prepare a regional conservation and development plan and budget, within the guidelines of the California State Plan.

The state zones are incorporated in the regional plan. The regional plan adopts limits for urban development in the regional reserve zone. In its open-space section, the plan specifies how the remaining open spaces in the regional reserve are to be protected.

To meet (or exceed) regional park minimum requirements, there is a program of park land acquisition and maintenance. The open-space section of the regional plan also adheres to other parts of the state plan, such as the minimum requirements for open space in urban neighborhoods. But the exact way that all this is done is decided after give-and-take among the regional planning agency, the municipalities, their community councils, private owners, and the general public. (All counties become municipalities under the structure of Driving Policy 1.)

To meet local open-space requirements, the plan of the people of one community might propose to convert many of the local streets to green strips, retaining only a bare essential of narrowed streets to allow for bus and other small local transit systems (in 1970, paved streets covered 30,000 acres of land in Santa Clara county).

Another community might convert vacant lots or those with decrepit houses into miniparks. Or a municipal plan could choose to purchase isolated houses in outlying areas, turn the outlying lands into greenspace, or even restore them as agricultural land, and concentrate development in the central districts.

The region takes all of these projects into account and makes an economic analysis of the total regional open-space program, and this, along with economic analyses in other action areas (housing, transportation, etc.), is used in drawing up the regional plan and budget (pages 53-55). The end result, once the regional government adopts a total program, the Congress authorizes the federal features of it, and the specified funding begins, is that all of the people of Santa Clara County can be assured of an extensive open-space preservation program, from every residential neighborhood to the surrounding hillsides. They know which open spaces are going to be preserved and for what purposes, when this is going to happen, and where the money is coming from.

**2. How can a pleasing and serviceable transportation system be developed in the Santa Barbara area?**

*Santa Barbara: transportation*

The Santa Barbara basin is subject to air inversions. As the number of automobiles increases, the area becomes very susceptible to smog. U. S. Highway 101, a major north-south route, runs through the west side of the city, as does the Southern Pacific's north-south rail line. The highway is subject to some congestion. It acts as a barrier which separates the downtown from the beach area, and generates noise and air pollution.

U. S. 101 serves as a link between Los Angeles and San Francisco, but a large part of its traffic comes from people traveling locally in the South Coast area. Because of a lack of low-income housing in Santa Barbara, many persons who work in the city live in the Carpinteria area and use U. S. 101 to travel to work. In addition, many faculty members and employees of the UC Santa Barbara campus at Goleta live south of Santa Barbara. There is no rapid bus or rail link between Santa Barbara, Carpinteria, and Goleta. Nor is there a satisfactory public-transit system linking various neighborhoods and outlying areas with the central business district or the beaches.

The state infrastructure plan of CALIFORNIA TWO would include a section on this area. The government of Region 7 (coastal counties, Santa Cruz to Santa Barbara) is required to include a transportation element in its comprehensive regional plan and budget. In assembling a transportation program, the regional planning agency might first suggest to the Santa Barbara municipalities (city and county) some general, alternative approaches to solving the transportation problems of the area.

The municipalities and the community councils would hold public hearings on the alternatives, and express their own planning objectives. In due course a preliminary regional plan, including the transportation section, would be published and subjected to public hearings in the counties. A final plan would be adopted by the regional legislature.

It might retain the old U. S. 101 at four lanes in width, underground in the downtown Santa Barbara area (State, Anacapa, and Santa Barbara streets would pass over the underground portion), and designate a new freeway-bypass route. The north-south Southern Pacific tracks might be designated for commuter train service along the coast. An improved local bus system would connect outlying areas with the city center, in keeping with state access standards.

The proposed system would, of course, be justified in planning and engineering studies. An economic feasibility study would accompany not only the proposed transportation program but the entire regional plan and program. Sources of funds—local, regional, state, federal and private—would all be specified so that regional and local budgets would be geared to the accomplishment of the program. Thus the piecemeal "solutions" of the past, imposed upon Santa Barbara by the state bureaucracy or by one or another local agency, are replaced by a comprehensive regional approach to planning and conservation closely related to the region, its citizens and their needs.

### 3. How can good health care be provided for all the citizens of a typical region?

*Regional
health care*

Under Driving Policy 3, the state establishes standards for regional and community health-care facilities and services (page 63). It develops programs to help the regions carry out the standards. The state standards aim for the finest medical care for all Californians at prices the society can afford to pay; readily accessible medical facilities throughout the state; a complete range of medical services, including psychiatry and social counseling, heart surgery, pediatrics, dentistry, and ophthalmology; and freedom of choice for doctors and patients who do not wish to participate in the health program.

Standards for the regions include specific requirements for major urban health facilities to handle an optimum of 250,000 persons each; rural "health stations" staffed by doctors or paramedics, with transportation to the nearest major health facility; and facilities for special services such as open-heart surgery, radiotherapy and neurosurgery. Staff requirements would be approximately one physician for every 1,000 residents, and three paramedics for every physician. Regions are encouraged to build biregional centers in areas where it would be impractical for either region to build a separate center.

Each region is responsible for preparing a health-care plan and budget, reflecting the state's standards, as part of its total conservation and development program. A typical regional health-care plan, developed in cooperation with the municipalities and community councils, would describe a complete system of health care, including the kinds and locations of specific health-care facilities. Facilities for a typical area would include:

- a fully equipped hospital for intensive care;
- a diagnostic center (or "going-in" hospital) where people could

be cared for inexpensively and, when possible, on a self-serve basis;
- a clinic for mental health and alcoholism;
- an extended-care facility for the aged and long-time convalescents;
- an attractive retirement home (located away from the hospital);
- a well-equipped research center.

There would be a training program for interns, residents, paramedics and doctors on a post-graduate level.

In rural areas, a health-care center would be centrally located so that it would be within 30 minutes' traveling time by helicopter of any point in the area. Small cities and towns would be served, in addition, by local clinics staffed by one or more doctors and several paramedical helpers. Major medical centers such as those operated by the University of California would provide specialized treatment facilities for groups of regions. To help achieve effective operation of its health program and to combat difficult health problems, the state carries on a variety of programs involving education, training, and clinical assistance.

The responsibility for financing, constructing and operating health facilities would be shared by the federal government, the state, the regions, and groups of physicians. A "going-in" hospital, for example, might be built by the region through a public corporation and operated by a group of private physicians under terms of a contract with the corporation. To assure that medical care is responsive to local concerns, such a contract might require that administrative policies of the facility be determined in cooperation with community councils.

The regions depend heavily on federal sources of financing—support for specific medical programs and new sources of general assistance to regions, such as those which would be provided by the Federal Conservation and Development Bank. A national program of medical insurance for individuals is essential to the operation of this or any universal health-care program. The costs of national health insurance are reasonable under an efficient regional health-care program (see economic analysis, page 99).

All aspects of the regional health program would be accounted for in the comprehensive regional plan and budget, to demonstrate once again to every citizen not only what kind of service he will receive, but when it will be instituted and how it will be paid for.

A tour of California Two

The foregoing examples show how the CALIFORNIA TWO structure might be capable of helping people solve actual problems in real places. The development of similar studies in all regions for all of the 21 disruptions identified on page 10 would begin to bring into focus a picture of life in CALIFORNIA TWO, as follows:

*Community building*

A community which, in the early 1970s, was part of an array of aging, run-down central-city homes, has now been largely redeemed in a regional renewal program carried out over more than two decades, step by logical step. Many homes and apartments have been renovated; others have been replaced; some have been removed to create neighborhood parks; the installation of new public transportation

INNER CITY
STREETS INTO
GARDENS

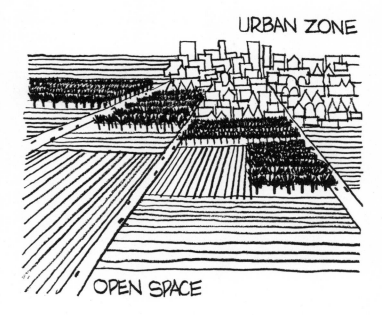

URBAN ZONE

OPEN SPACE

facilities in the area has permitted some streets to be closed off and turned into playgrounds or gardens. New clusters of offices and stores, churches and meeting places have sprung up around the transit stops. The area is safer and far more pleasant than most communities were in the past.

The old, established cities are still sprawled out, but not much more than they were in the 1970s. They come to a stop at their boundaries, at the edge of the urban zone, and beyond that there is farmland or undeveloped hills.

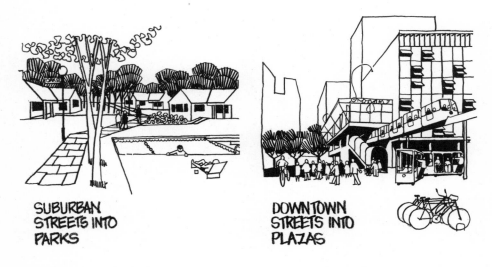

SUBURBAN STREETS INTO PARKS

DOWNTOWN STREETS INTO PLAZAS

The shape of a community is determined in good measure by what people want. The community council has a strong voice in city and county planning. Decisions must be in keeping with the regional plan and the priorities of the regional budget. There are practical considerations, such as the financing available from the Federal Conservation and Development Bank and other sources. Nevertheless, local imagination and preference come through. The big-city communities are quite different from one another in size, in layout, in architectural appearance, and in other characteristics.

All housing has to be within standards set by the California State Plan. These deal with such matters as the availability of housing to all income groups; accessibility to work, shopping, recreation and health care; amounts of private and public open space provided; and quality of construction.

The population has leveled off at about 30 million, an increase of ten million since 1970. New cities have absorbed some of these people, but most of them have been accommodated in existing urban areas. Also, rural assistance programs have encouraged people to stay on the land.

Because of the pattern of concentrated urban development in CALIFORNIA TWO, government does not have to extend municipal services such as water-supply and waste-disposal facilities into every corner of the far countryside. State conservation and agricultural

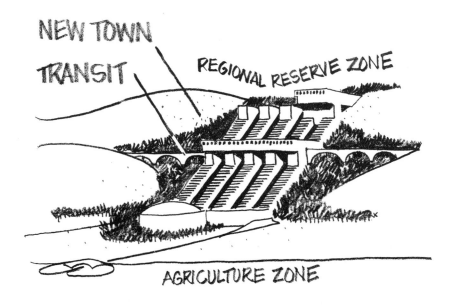

zones are not open to urban development. Many regional-reserve lands are left open or in low-density housing, by choice of the regions.

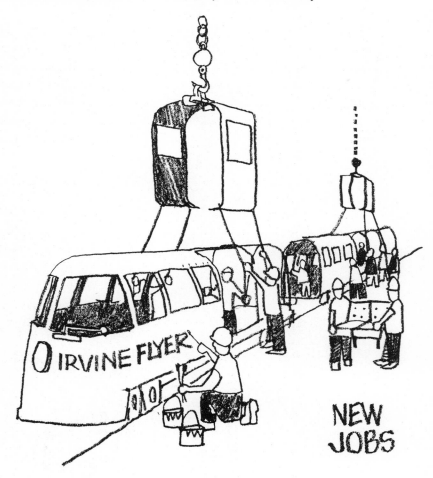

*Making a living*

A wide choice among residential locations is now available to those who, in the past, could not afford to move out of neighborhoods they did not like. This results from expanded job opportunities, a guaranteed income floor, and new or renewed housing which meets "California Standards" of amenity and availability.

Because of the income floor, people are not locked into dead-end employment, nor do they have to face the specter of prolonged unemployment or dependency on relief. They do not need to fight or train for jobs which are not available. At the same time, the income floor is not munificent, and most people want to work and have the opportunity of working. There are a great many jobs offered, year after year, as each additional increment to the major regional development programs is built. These multibillion-dollar programs provide employment directly, and also cause many more jobs to be created in support industries and services. The state encourages other kinds of development in keeping with the goals of the California State Plan. The state-wide employment-information network brings early warning to the local schools and training institutions of what skills will be needed.

*Schools for the community*

The schools are centers of year-round study and they inspire all kinds of avocational and recreational activity. Activities formerly considered "hobbies," such as fine craftsmanship or organic gardening, have become full-time pursuits. Under the regional development program, schools at all levels become centers of community life. Their libraries, classes, electronic equipment, their spirit of awakening, serve not only students but all the people of the area.

COMMUNITY CENTER

*Health care*

There is a complete system of health care. Everyone is covered by the national health program. The option of choosing a private doctor is open, but there is a publicly provided health clinic for every community, and a regional system of hospitals and care programs for the aged and mentally ill. The community councils help determine the character of each local clinic. The cost to society of providing adequate health care is high.

*Public transportation for the regions*

Public transportation forms the skeleton of entire urban regions. Regional transportation systems are based on a combination of rapid-transit lines of various kinds—minirail, computer-controlled jitneys, buses, other feeder vehicles and "people moving" conveyances in commercial centers or neighborhood residential areas. Nonpolluting automobiles are used extensively, but it is not necessary for individuals to own automobiles; there are attractive alternatives.

Transit systems provide good service for entire cities and may include a concentrated grid covering 100 square miles or more in sprawling areas like Los Angeles, with high-speed connectors to other com-

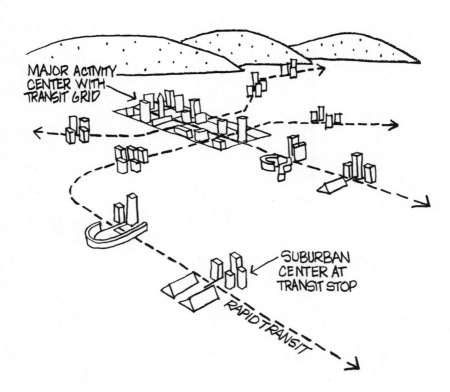

MAJOR ACTIVITY CENTER WITH TRANSIT GRID

SUBURBAN CENTER AT TRANSIT STOP

RAPID TRANSIT

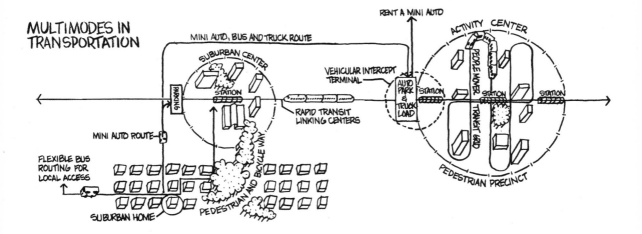

**MULTIMODES IN TRANSPORTATION**

RENT A MINI AUTO

MINI AUTO, BUS AND TRUCK ROUTE

SUBURBAN CENTER

ACTIVITY CENTER

VEHICULAR INTERCEPT TERMINAL

PARKING

STATION

AUTO PARK & TRUCK LOAD

STATION

PEOPLE MOVER TRANSIT GRID

STATION

STATION

RAPID TRANSIT LINKING CENTERS

MINI AUTO ROUTE

FLEXIBLE BUS ROUTING FOR LOCAL ACCESS

PEDESTRIAN AND BICYCLE WAY

PEDESTRIAN PRECINCT

SUBURBAN HOME

munities in the region. The regional transportation system is an integral part of the regional plan and is used as a basis for areawide renewal. It makes possible, for example, the conversion in large sections of Los Angeles of over half the established street grid, including freeways that existed in California Zero, to greenways of various kinds. The planning possibilities, right down to the residential neighborhood level, are exciting when the established street grid of California Zero can be regarded not simply as a paved-over runway for cars but as a public resource of almost limitless opportunity.

The transit stations become centers of activity—stores, offices, health facilities, some apartments, places of worship, recreational areas, plazas, theaters, meeting places. The land surrounding the transit stations is acquired, as part of the right-of-way purchase, by the public corporation which has been chartered by the regional government to assist in carrying out the regional development program. Income derived from these areas helps to retire the construction loans. In addition, these funds help to create community facilities, such as schools, which are part of the total regional plan.

The full-coverage aspect of the regional transportation system corresponds to a trend away from the commuting patterns of the past when citizens jammed the freeways to get from their homes in one place to high-rise urban centers in another. Many activities now revolve around local centers. And new or improved forms of electronic communication bring people together sufficiently well so that they do not have to travel to be in proximity with each other.

There is a new ultra-high-speed rail line linking the northern and southern parts of the state. Along this rail line are new cities designed to take the pressure off the urban clusters centering around old city cores.

High-speed rail line can travel through regional-reserve lands

*Environmental quality*

The open spaces of California are protected. The map (page 58) shows the extent of the conservation, agricultural and regional-reserve zones. The state conservation zone includes most of the lands which are of major scenic and recreational importance, such as the entire coastline and important mountain and desert regions.

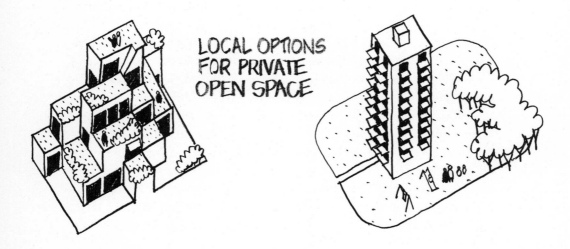

LOCAL OPTIONS FOR PRIVATE OPEN SPACE

HARBOR
WATERS

The infusion of open-space recreational areas into every community, under the state and regional standards, helps to make the city a good place to be, instead of a good place to get away from.

In CALIFORNIA TWO, some of the most important environmental concerns of past decades have diminished. However, development of new, clean energy sources remains a concern, and the search for them is strongly accelerated. Air and water quality now meet the high California Standards for amenity, polluters having been guided and encouraged by the state consumption policies into new ways of operation. Very few of the old, ecologically destructive interbasin water-diversion proposals have been carried out since the early 1970s. The regions produce much of their own water through recycling, desalinization and judicious tapping of underground supplies.

Systematic collection and disposal of solid wastes are part of each regional development plan and are financed within the total regional development program. Waste facilities can handle completely, efficiently and economically, without pollution and without the depletion involved in extensive land fill, all of the solid wastes of the region through separation into components suitable for direct reuse, recycling, conversion to new materials, or combustion with steam production.

People do not have a great deal of disposable income, and costs are high, partly because of the environmental constraints on manufacturers. Taxes are high. But new buying habits, guaranteed public access to amenities such as public transportation and parks, clean air and water, and health-care services stand in lieu of direct purchasing power. Most people eat better and enjoy better housing than they could have years before.

There is still crime, drug abuse, and disorder, but regional programs of rehabilitation in CALIFORNIA TWO have replaced the primitive approach of the past. Crime and other social disruptions are at more tolerable levels, at least in part because many of the conditions which used to cause them—poverty, hunger, poor housing, and blighted neighborhoods—have been alleviated.

Still, many are discontented—with housing, income, and restrictions on the use of private property. Prejudice, and inequities arising from it, are still on the scene. Nevertheless, the restructuring of the planning process gives citizens a chance to work with the governmental bodies—community, regional, and state—which are actually responsible for solving important problems.

There are widespread complaints about government interference, bureaucratic red tape and waste of money. In actual fact, government exerts strong controls mainly in the areas that are necessary for the protection of the natural environment. In other areas, government helps to establish a framework under which individuals and communities can decide pretty much for themselves how they want to live their lives on the land.

In other words, CALIFORNIA TWO is not to be considered Utopia, but a reasonable, workable conception of how planning can help assure that this state and this nation will be better places for people to live, rather than worse, in the decades ahead.

# Comparisons of
# California One
# and California Two

# Comparisons of California One and California Two

All told, how do CALIFORNIA ONE and CALIFORNIA TWO compare, one against the other?

*Problem solving*

It is clear that **California One** fails to provide effective, long-term answers to the state's social and environmental problems. Responsibility for solving state and regional problems remains divided among local governments with narrow jurisdictions and distant state and federal agencies. Single-purpose agencies still pursue their separate policies and programs with little concern for the effects of their decisions on policies and programs in other problem areas. The programs of CALIFORNIA ONE are, typically, palliatives which ignore underlying causes of disruption. So-called remedies intensify original problems and create new ones. Public frustration increases with the government's inability to improve the quality of life. People see few avenues of influence open to them, and feel that they and their neighborhoods have been forgotten.

**California Two** avoids the increasing problems and frustrations of CALIFORNIA ONE by adopting a wide-ranging state plan for the future and by instituting new government procedures and structures far more responsive to people and their needs. The plan, with four driving policies related to four identified causes of disruption, guides the design of both government structure and operational policy. Conflicting single-purpose agencies, policies and programs are replaced by coordinated agencies, all directed toward achieving the resolution of California's problems. The planning process becomes visible and accessible, less subject to political manipulation. Individuals have new opportunities for personal fulfillment, and the state adheres to high standards of environmental amenity.

*Economic questions*

There are, in addition, vital economic questions. How would the economies of the two Californias affect the land and the people of the state? What would the two Californias cost?

California Two removes problems by grouping policies to deal with causes.

## DISRUPTIONS

**LAND/AIR/WATER**
1. Energy resources
2. Water sources
3. Wild lands & open spaces
4. Agricultural land
5. Species
6. Air quality
7. Water quality
8. Noise
9. Visual order

**STRUCTURES**
10. Transportation
11. Energy distribution & communications
12. Solid waste
13. Disaster-prone structures
14. Housing
15. Community facilities

**PEOPLE**
16. Employment
17. Education
18. Health
19. Recreation
20. Civil order
21. Security

## POLICIES

- PROVIDE POLITICAL STRENGTH
- PROVIDE ECONOMIC STRENGTH
- GUIDE SETTLEMENT
- GUIDE RESOURCE USE

## CAUSES

- Lack of individual political strength
- Lack of individual economic strength
- Damaging distribution of population
- Damaging patterns of resource consumption

Sets of connected policies are directed at underlying causes of disruptions

● Major policies

In **California One,** policies that encourage unrestrained economic growth result in increased urbanization and environmental destruction. Government contributes to this process by subsidizing many enterprises, both directly and indirectly, and by only sporadically enforcing control regulations. Economic growth in CALIFORNIA ONE provides jobs, but in many instances in enterprises which have destructive impact on the environment and on people. The job market is highly unpredictable.

The state budget continues to reflect the separate programs of single-purpose agencies. The state budgeting and accounting process is not geared to making full assessments of the costs and benefits, direct and indirect, of various planning alternatives. As the problems of CALIFORNIA ONE get worse, the costs of doing business increase to overwhelming proportions in every area, including government.

**California Two** replaces the antiquated notion of unrestrained economic growth with a modern concept of a strong economy within an amenable environment. It encourages economic development; a thriving economy is essential to the implementation of the state's driving policies. But CALIFORNIA TWO also guides the consumption of energy, space, and certain commodities, in order to maintain a permanently pleasant and productive environment in the state. Private enterprise continues to produce a wide range of goods and services, within environmental limits clearly defined in the California State Plan.

Wasteful government spending is reduced through the reorganization of government agencies, the coordination of programs at all levels, and the adoption of new budgeting and planning procedures which identify the costs and benefits of alternative programs. Through

# California One attacks symptoms

| SINGLE-PURPOSE POLICIES DIRECTED AT DISRUPTION EFFECTS | DISRUPTIONS | | |
|---|---|---|---|
| | **LAND/AIR/WATER** | **STRUCTURES** | **PEOPLE** |
| | 1. Energy resources ● <br> 2. Water sources ● <br> 3. Wild lands & open spaces ● <br> 4. Agricultural land ● <br> 5. Species ● <br> 6. Air quality ● <br> 7. Water quality ● <br> 8. Noise ● <br> 9. Visual order ● | 10. Transportation ● <br> 11. Energy distribution & communications ● <br> 12. Solid waste ● <br> 13. Disaster-prone structures ● <br> 14. Housing ● <br> 15. Community facilities ● | 16. Employment ● <br> 17. Education ● <br> 18. Health ● <br> 19. Recreation ● <br> 20. Civil order ● <br> 21. Security ● |

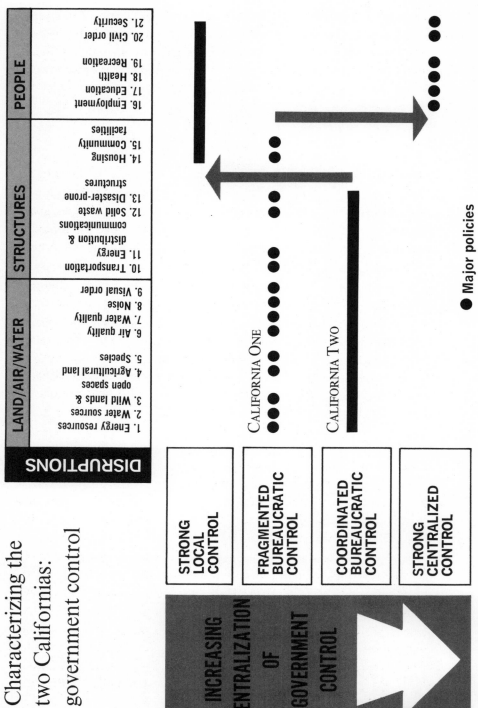

Characterizing the two Californias: government control

its economic development policies, including programs of manpower development, regional renewal and pollution control, CALIFORNIA Two provides a setting in which there can be an adequate and steady supply of jobs. It demonstrates that economic sufficiency can be maintained without destroying the environment in the process.

## An examination of costs

In order to gain an insight into the respective costs of CALIFORNIAS ONE and TWO, we have developed cost comparisons of alternative approaches to problems in three specific areas of concern—open space, transportation and health care. In doing so, we have attempted to estimate both the direct and indirect costs of each alternative. A complete benefit-cost analysis comparing CALIFORNIA ONE and CALIFORNIA Two is not possible within the scope of this plan, but the examples give some indications of the costs of each. We have used the most reliable data available, recognizing the existence of many unknowns. Nevertheless, these are realistic estimates of the magnitude of costs implied by each alternative. Furthermore, they indicate the kinds of considerations that must be included in future budgeting and accounting processes if the true costs and benefits of various courses of action are to be determined.

*Costs:*
*open space*
CALIFORNIA TWO would preserve agricultural lands, wildlife habitats, areas of scenic and historical interest, watersheds, and zones especially subject to natural hazards such as earthquake, fire and flood. Most of this land would be secured through statewide zoning regulations. Some would be purchased outright or in less-than-fee by public agencies. Land would be taxed according to its zoning classification.

We estimated the costs of a statewide open-space program by using the cost figures developed in 1969 in a landmark study of the "Economic Impact of a Regional Open Space Program" for the Bay Area. The study was commissioned by a group called People for Open Space (POS), with assistance from the Ford Foundation. We applied these figures to the state's urban open-space requirements projected in "The Urban Metropolitan Open Space Study" prepared by Eckbo, Dean, Austin and Williams (EDAW) for the State Office of Planning in 1965.

Of the more than nine million acres of open space within and adjacent to the metropolitan centers of California, the EDAW study recommends that 20 percent, or 1.8 million acres, be secured through full- or partial-fee acquisition. The study estimates the acquisition cost of this land in 1970 dollars to be about $4.0 billion. Assuming five-percent, 30-year bonds, yearly amortization payments would average about $260 million.

Expressed in constant 1970 dollars, the annual cost in the year 2000 of administering and maintaining the total open-space program —including the development of a considerable amount of new park land—would approximate $30 million.

Therefore, the total annual cost of an open-space program would be about $290 million.

The POS study discovered, incidentally, that the designation of large areas of bay region land as permanent open space would not result in any appreciable decrease in the yield of tax revenues within the region. According to the study, "the gains in values of urban land and developable land not included in the open space plan would approximate the loss in values in the open space lands."

In estimating CALIFORNIA ONE costs, we have assumed that 50 percent of the urban open space proposed for protection in the EDAW study would be developed by the year 2000.

*Concentrated development lowers costs*

The POS study discovered that it costs more to provide utilities and government services to residents in low-density suburban areas than it does to provide these services to the same number of residents in existing urban areas. The difference in these two costs is one of the public costs of suburban development; it is borne by the public in the form of higher utility rates and higher taxes. With figures developed in the POS study, it can be estimated that the total additional cost of extending gas, electricity, water and telephone lines to 50 percent of the open-space land in and around California's major metropolitan areas would approximate $5.2 billion. Averaged over a 30-year period, the annual cost would be $173 million. The additional cost of maintaining these utilities over the same period would be about $84 million a year. Assuming that such costs would be financed by five-percent, 30-year bonds, interest charges would average $260 million a year. Thus, the annual additional cost of bringing utilities to these lands, as opposed to providing them in existing urban areas, would be $517 million. The additional cost of establishing governmental services within the newly developed areas would bring the total annual cost of development under CALIFORNIA ONE to $684 million.

## Open space *vs.* added costs of low-density development—a summary

### CALIFORNIA ONE

*Annual cost of:*

|  |  |
|---|---|
| Extending utilities | $173 million |
| Maintaining additional utilities | 84 million |
| Interest on utilities investment | 260 million |
| Providing governmental services | 167 million |
| Total annual cost of development | $684 million |

### CALIFORNIA TWO

*Annual cost of:*

|  |  |
|---|---|
| Land acquisition (including interest payments) | $260 million |
| Administration and maintenance in the year 2000 | 30 million |
| Total annual cost of providing open space | $290 million |

*(Figures shown are in 1970 dollars.)*

*Costs: transportation in the Los Angeles area*

We have chosen five Southern California counties—Los Angeles, Orange, Riverside, San Bernardino, and Ventura—for an illustration of the costs associated with our current automobile/freeway-dominated transportation system, augmented by some mass transit, as compared to the cost of implementing in the same area a more complete multi-mode transportation network.

CALIFORNIA ONE would continue to rely on the automobile and the freeway system to serve major transportation needs. Problems associated with automobile use—smog, congestion, noise, traffic accidents, etc., would continue. Most people would find using an automobile either mandatory or more convenient than depending on other forms of transportation. Nevertheless, for the purposes of our study, we assume that under CALIFORNIA ONE the Southern California Rapid

Transit District would install by the year 2000 the five-corridor mass-transit system outlined in its master plan. This system would consist of 89 miles of double-track rapid transit along the five existing major traffic corridors. It would be augmented by 850 additional buses and 300 miles of new bus lines to feed the system. SCRTD estimates the total cost of installing this system at $2.5 billion. Even with the system in operation, the remaining volume of traffic is expected to require the construction of an additional 1,000 miles of new freeway, representing a further capital investment of $8 billion.

In CALIFORNIA TWO, state, regional and local governments would begin to take steps to provide alternate and economical means of transportation for all residents. Each region in the state would assess its transportation needs and conduct benefit/cost analyses of alternate transit proposals designed to meet these needs. CALIFORNIA TWO would not eliminate the automobile, but it would provide people with convenient alternatives and with inducements to use them.

*A major transit installation*

No designs or costs exist for a regional, integrated transportation system in the five-county study area, but for purposes of discussion we can imagine for CALIFORNIA TWO a rapid-transit grid covering 100 square miles of central Los Angeles, high-speed lines offering service comparable to that proposed by SCRTD reaching into the outlying areas, a complete feeder-bus program twice the size of that proposed by SCRTD, 500 miles of new freeways, and other transportation components throughout the region. Proposals for a central transit grid may or may not be appropriate for the area but, by using available cost estimates associated with it and the other components, we can develop preliminary cost estimates for the kind of multimode regional transportation program which CALIFORNIA TWO makes possible.

A transit grid for 100 square miles of central Los Angeles would put a single-track, rapid-transit loop within one-half mile of any point on the grid. The system would require 258 miles of track and 200 platforms within the grid. In addition, there would be 120 miles of track to outlying areas. Assuming the use of existing rights-of-way, and considering the greatly reduced costs of installing single-track as opposed to double-track lines, we can estimate that such a system, together with a complete feeder-bus program twice the size of that proposed by SCRTD, could be installed for a total capital investment of $4.5 billion, probably eliminating the need for half the additional freeways proposed for CALIFORNIA ONE. Thus, CALIFORNIA TWO freeway-construction costs would approximate $4 billion. In addition, another

$2 billion could be spent on multimode transportation components throughout the region without exceeding the CALIFORNIA ONE expenditures.

With regard to annual operating costs for each of the two different systems, SCRTD estimates the annual cost of operation and maintenance of their system at $50 million; the operation of the CALIFORNIA TWO transit system is estimated at $225 million a year. The costs of maintaining roadways under CALIFORNIA ONE and CALIFORNIA TWO are included below in the discussion of automobile costs.

*Automobile costs usually understated*

The major difference between the two systems appears when we consider the annual cost to the public of continued reliance on the automobile under CALIFORNIA ONE. Traditionally, automobile costs have been understated because only direct costs have been considered. Mass-transit costs have been overstated because indirect benefits have been ignored. The development of mass transit in large part depends on the public's awareness of the real cost of the auto-dominated transportation system.

Using available data and methods developed in recent transportation and environment studies, we can approximate the real costs—direct and indirect—of continued reliance on the automobile in the five Southern California counties, where the problems associated with automobile use are most acute.

The American Automobile Association estimates the average, annual, out-of-pocket costs of driving an automobile, based on a 10,000-mile year, at $1,550. These include the purchase price (spread over five years) and the costs of financing, depreciation, insurance, fuel, parking, and maintenance. To this basic figure, the Rapid Transit Society located in San Jose adds $800 to cover such costs as property taxes diverted to highway construction and maintenance, the loss of property taxes on the land beneath roads, and a part of the amount added to the price of a house for tract streets and garages, for a total of $2,350 a year. This figure, multiplied by the number of automobiles in the five-county study area, produces the estimated cost of auto ownership in the area in 1970: $14.6 billion.

To this figure must be added annual costs of maintaining parking spaces and roads, of significant damage to health and property from air pollution, and of lost time spent in traffic tie-ups.

Drawing on figures developed in Stanford Research Institute's 1968 "Benefit/Cost Analysis of the Five-Corridor Rapid Transit System for Los Angeles," we can estimate the annual cost of maintaining parking facilities in the five-county area to be approximately $634 million.

According to the "California Statistical Abstract/1970," the annual cost of road maintenance in the five counties was $871 million. This figure, of course, is now higher because of inflation and the increased number of automobiles.

The annual cost of air pollution in the Los Angeles air basin has been estimated by Ralph d'Arge, an economist at the University of California, Riverside, to be $336 million.

The Stanford Research Institute has estimated the value of one hour of a driver's time during peak traffic periods to be $2.82. In 1970, the time spent driving in "rush-hour traffic" in the five counties amounted to 482 million hours. Therefore, the cost of this time totaled $1.36 billion.

The total, annual cost of the automobile/freeway transportation system in the five counties in 1970 was about $17.8 billion. This figure does not include a number of other costs.

*Annual cost of the automobile in the year 2000*

The total cost figure can be projected to the year 2000, using population estimates, based on the 1970 census, developed by the Population Research Unit of the State Department of Finance. Such a projection assumes that the ratio of automobiles to people would remain constant and that automobile costs would remain proportionate to the number of vehicles on the road. Air-pollution costs are discounted to allow for predicted improvements in emission levels. The projected costs are stated in 1970 dollars, but actual costs would be higher than indicated because of inflation.

The total annual cost of continued, virtually complete reliance on the automobile for transportation in the five Southern California counties in the year 2000 is estimated to be $27.9 billion.

However, SCRTD estimates that its five-corridor rapid-transit system could reduce the total annual volume of automobile traffic by ten percent and auto ownership by nearly two percent. Assuming this figure, in CALIFORNIA ONE in the year 2000, the remaining 9.7 million automobiles would travel 88.9 billion miles. The costs of auto ownership and maintenance would be $21.2 billion. Assuming that costs of air pollution, parking and roadway maintenance, and lost travel time would be cut by ten percent, the annual cost of the CALIFORNIA ONE transportation system would be approximately $25.5 billion.

The CALIFORNIA TWO transportation network would include many more true alternatives to private automobile travel than the CALI-

FORNIA ONE system. It would be serviced by more transit lines, more buses, and by additional multimode transit throughout the region. Its use would be encouraged by various incentives such as those outlined in Driving Policy 4. These include a tax on automobiles to cover the costs of their recycling, and an oil-depletion tax. It may be necessary in CALIFORNIA TWO, in order to provide transportation systems that are convenient, economical and environmentally sound, to employ still other inducements. For example, automobiles might be taxed to defray the costs of solving problems such as air pollution and urban congestion which are directly connected to automobile use. Such costs are now borne by drivers and nondrivers alike.

*Annual cost of the California Two system in the year 2000*

Supported by these kinds of incentives, the CALIFORNIA TWO transportation network could be expected to reduce the annual volume of traffic by 20 percent and automobile ownership by seven percent. This would cut total annual automobile ownership and operating costs to $18.5 billion and would reduce other auto-associated costs by 20 percent. Thus, the estimated total annual cost of the CALIFORNIA TWO transportation system in the year 2000 is $22.2 billion. These figures suggest that we can undertake far-reaching solutions to our transportation problems and still spend less than if we continue to rely on the automobile as the basic mode of intraregional transport.

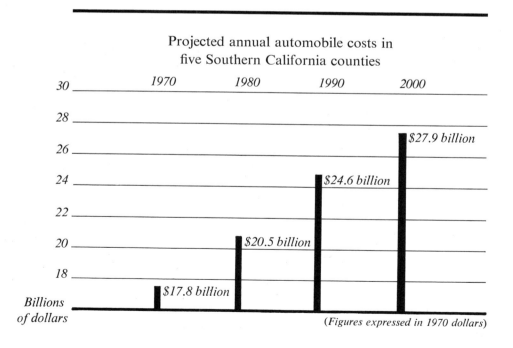

Projected annual automobile costs in
five Southern California counties

| 1970 | 1980 | 1990 | 2000 |

30

28

26 — $27.9 billion

24 — $24.6 billion

22

20 — $20.5 billion

18

$17.8 billion

*Billions of dollars*

*(Figures expressed in 1970 dollars)*

# Two approaches to transportation—a summary

| ITEM | CALIFORNIA ONE | CALIFORNIA TWO |
|---|---|---|
| Transit system installation | $2,500 million | $6,500 million |
| Freeway construction | 8,000 million | 4,000 million |

ANNUAL EXPENSES BY 2000

| | CALIFORNIA ONE | CALIFORNIA TWO |
|---|---|---|
| Transit system operation | $50 million | $225 million |
| Auto ownership and operating expenses | 21,226 million | 18,530 million |
| Maintenance of parking spaces | 895 million | 796 million |
| Maintenance of roads | 1,230 million | 1,094 million |
| Air-pollution costs (including projected improvements) | 180 million | 160 million |
| Lost travel time | 1,922 million | 1,708 million |
| *Total* | $25,503 million | $22,513 million |

*(Figures shown are in 1970 dollars.)*

From 1966 to 1971, national health-care expenditures increased from $42 billion to $75 billion annually and per-capita expenditures from $212 to $358. Sixty percent of this increase was due to inflation. Other contributing factors were the increase in population and in the portion of the population over 65 years of age, and the extension of government-financed health programs to persons who formerly received inadequate medical care. Government programs and private health insurance together account for less than 65 percent of the total annual health expenditures. Hence, out-of-pocket medical expenditures in 1971 averaged about $11 per month per person. Given expected population increases and the likely continuation of trends affecting health costs, the total national health-care expenditures in the year 2000 will be about $280 billion, and per-capita costs will have nearly tripled. This amount will be reached without any extension of the current scope of medical care or change in the method of delivering health services.

*A limited*
*program*

In CALIFORNIA ONE, with a projected population of 32 million in the year 2000, medical expenditures would total about $31 billion a year. We can estimate that two-thirds of this amount would be covered by a national program of health insurance. Perhaps as much as 18 percent of the total would be paid by private insurance policies. A national program of this scale would barely cover the annual costs of hospital care, physicians' fees, and the construction of new facilities. The individual would still pay as he was able for all dental and other professional services, all drugs, eyeglasses and other appliances, and nursing-home care. Furthermore, the poor would continue to have to seek out assembly-line care at hospitals distant from their homes. Many community clinics would continue to require private funding for support.

*A comprehensive*
*program*

In projecting the costs of a comprehensive health-care program under CALIFORNIA TWO, we can begin with the costs associated with the Kaiser Plan. In 1971, the per-capita cost of care under this plan averaged $180. The Kaiser Plan, however, does not accommodate the totally disabled or the elderly. With the help of figures developed by the Health Manpower Commission of 1967, it can be estimated that the extension of care to these groups would increase the per-capita cost under the plan to about $270 per year. Assuming that this amount would increase in the future at the same rate as medical costs in general, the annual per-capita cost of basic medical care under CALIFORNIA TWO would be about $700, as compared to $935 under CALIFORNIA

# Health care in the year 2000—a summary

|  | CALIFORNIA ONE | CALIFORNIA TWO |
|---|---|---|
| *Total cost of health care* | $31 billion | $30 billion |
| *Public expenditure* | 21 billion | 29 billion |
| *Private expenditure* | 10 billion | 1 billion |

(*Figures shown are in 1970 dollars.*)

| *Health-care services provided:* | | |
|---|---|---|
| *Public expenditure* | Hospital care<br>Physicians' fees<br>Laboratory fees<br>Surgery | All health-care services, including dental care, mental-health care, nursing homes, physical therapy, drugs, eyeglasses, hearing aids, prosthetic devices, kidney machines, etc. |
| *Private expenditure* | Dental care<br>Mental-health care<br>Nursing homes<br>Physical therapy<br>Drugs and medical appliances<br>Other professional services | Limited to those individuals who prefer to seek private medical care. |
| *Who receives complete medical care?* | Those who can pay for the medical services **not** covered by government health insurance. | Anyone who needs it. |

ONE. On the basis of Great Britain's experience with its comprehensive health-care program, it can be assumed that 98 percent of the CALIFORNIA TWO population of 30 million would participate.

The estimated total cost of basic medical services for 24.4 million people in the year 2000 would be $20.6 billion.

But the program proposed under CALIFORNIA TWO would expand the services currently offered under the Kaiser Plan to a full range of health needs. Therefore, we must add to the total expenditure for a basic program the costs of doctors' visits, dental care, and the support of nursing homes, and expenditures for mental hygiene. Assuming that the costs of all these services continue to increase at current rates, we must add $8.4 billion to the cost of the basic program for these additional services.

Although the health-care program in CALIFORNIA TWO would offer complete medical care to everyone, it is to be expected that some people would prefer to make additional expenditures for private care. Assuming that two percent of the projected population of 30 million would prefer to continue private medical care, private health care would add an estimated $300 million to the CALIFORNIA TWO program, bringing the annual total for the program to $29.3 billion.

Thus, the CALIFORNIA TWO health-care program would provide full medical care at modern, conveniently located centers for less than the projected costs of health under CALIFORNIA ONE. This extension of service at less cost is made possible by the reduced state population under CALIFORNIA TWO and by the significant economies resulting from large, coordinated, group medical practices. Furthermore, the projected costs of health care under CALIFORNIA TWO do not take into account the savings that would accrue from the general improvement of the health of our citizens.

## Amenities

The foregoing economic comparisons of CALIFORNIA ONE and CALIFORNIA TWO approaches to three specific problems suggest that we can achieve and pay for a better future than we are likely to get if present decision-making trends continue. The comparative values of these alternatives, however, can be only partly expressed in terms of dollars. The quality of life, after all, is what CALIFORNIA TWO is really about, and any comparison of the two Californias would be incomplete without a note about the amenities that each would provide.

Amenity values can sometimes be expressed in dollar amounts, such as the substantial savings that would accrue from the elimination of air pollution. It may be possible, in addition, to develop a system of measuring certain amenity benefits accruing to individuals (units of amenity value, or "U-haves") as an aid to decision-makers who must make full evaluations of the effects of alternative courses of action, and be able to justify their decisions. Some amenities, however, such as the pleasure of seeing wintering ducks on a country pond or of being able to see for miles on a hot summer day, are not so easily converted to numerical equivalents. Nor should they be. What precise dollar values, ultimately, can be put on maintaining and preserving the delicate ecosystems that keep us alive on "spaceship earth?"

CALIFORNIA ONE would not be without amenities, but most people, whatever their incomes, would find the quality of their lives rapidly deteriorating. Their cities would be noisier and more crowded with cars; their air and water dirtier; their recreational opportunities more limited; their taxes and costs of living higher; their countryside defaced.

Consider the following: before World War II, a middle-income family that wanted to live in the suburbs could afford a detached home with an ample if not generous yard on a quiet, well-planted residential street. After the war, the suburban pattern was mainly defined by the Levittown concept—narrower yards, smaller rooms with lower ceilings, token street planting, and little privacy. During the 1960s, cluster housing came into vogue, offering to compensate for the absence of private yards with common open spaces. Now these amenities are not often available: the usual garden apartment offers little of either garden or apartment. At the same time, the rapid spread of mobile homes provides a clue to the future of lower- and middle-income housing. The trend is obvious and disheartening, not only in the homes we live in, but in the air we breathe, the water we drink, the food we eat, the clothing we wear, the kinds of recreation we enjoy, the way we move from place to place and what we see along the way, the health care we receive, and the schools we send our children to.

CALIFORNIA TWO would arrest and reverse this trend.

# Phasing In—
# California Two

# Phasing In—
# California Two

This section considers the question of how to bring CALIFORNIA TWO into being. As we have shown earlier, the state is already moving toward CALIFORNIA ONE, which is based on a logical extension of present trends. Many of the policies of CALIFORNIA ONE are either in effect or in the planning stage.

Shifting direction toward CALIFORNIA TWO is another matter entirely, for it requires major changes in governmental structures, new levels and patterns of public and private spending, large-scale action programs, some new thinking, even new ways of life. Yet CALIFORNIA TWO or any other reasonable set of choices about the future can be achieved.

*Nine essential "activators"*

We have approached the achievement of CALIFORNIA TWO through nine basic "activators," which are listed below. Adoption of the activators, whether all at once through a sweeping legislative change, or more gradually, is simply a prerequisite for achieving the goals of CALIFORNIA TWO. The activators set up procedures for planning, programming, and budgeting, long-range as well as short-range, by which the vital needs and desires of the public can be attained.

Each CALIFORNIA TWO activator is of manageable size for political adoption. The adoption of each is in itself desirable and does not depend on the immediate adoption of the others. Furthermore, the activators need not be put into effect in the order listed. They can all be advanced at once, or any one at a time. Nevertheless, together they constitute the essentials of a complete system capable of operating effectively.

It must be emphasized that the full strength and purpose of the activators cannot be compromised. The demands of the political process may require that the activators be broken down into smaller action units. But halfway measures which undermine and defeat any activator are unacceptable. They are worse than no action at all, for they preempt the field. For example, the creation, year after year, of new single-purpose regional commissions in California would begin to get in the way of achieving activator 4—the creation of multipurpose regional governments for every region in the state. In fact, we must guard against any narrowly conceived "solution" to California's problems. The test should be: "Is this proposal part of a comprehensive plan for solving problems and, if so, what is the plan and where does the proposal fit in?"

The activators are:

**1. Take emergency action** to protect valuable lands of the state that are in critical danger of change or destruction. The procedure involves rapid and complete identification of the endangered areas by the State Office of Planning and Research, and enactment by the legislature of emergency open-space zoning for the endangered lands. Such zoning would remain in effect pending the adoption of a full state zoning plan and other measures reflecting comprehensive state policies for settlement and resource use. (The CALIFORNIA TWO model of such policies can be found in the sections on Driving Policy 3 and Driving Policy 4, with a description of a state zoning plan on pages 57 to 59.)

**2. Adopt basic policies.** The legislature can identify and adopt central, driving policies for the state of California. The driving policies would form the basis for developing and coordinating all state policies and programs. (The CALIFORNIA TWO narrative proposes four driving policies, page 41, which could be a good starting point for the legislative discussion. The CALIFORNIA TWO narrative also shows how all major state policies can be organized around the driving policies.)

**3. Set up state planning and budgeting in one strong agency.** Such an agency would be required to produce a plan for the future of California—a California State Plan—within 18 months, and the plan would include corresponding long-term and yearly budgets. (A model state planning structure is outlined in the CALIFORNIA TWO narrative, pages 43 to 50. In fact, taken as a whole, the CALIFORNIA TWO narrative represents such a comprehensive state plan.)

**4. Establish regional governments.** Strong regional governments are absolutely essential to the operation of CALIFORNIA TWO. To give all Californians, residents of metropolitan and outlying areas alike, representation at the regional level, the legislature can establish major regional subdivisions of the state, set up the organization for a multipurpose government for each region, assign responsibilities to regional government, and provide for the necessary funding. (The CALIFORNIA TWO narrative offers a model for regional government in California, and a method of financing comprehensive regional improvement programs, pages 46 to 50.)

**5. Establish community councils.** The legislature can require the establishment of community councils within the framework of local government in order to give strong voice to neighborhood needs and concerns (see CALIFORNIA TWO, page 49).

**6. Make new election laws** to prevent the election process from being overwhelmed by special, powerful, economic interests (see CALIFORNIA TWO, page 50).

**7. Use modern fact-gathering techniques.** The legislature can assure the financing necessary to develop a model of the state's social and economic conditions and resource capabilities, as an essential tool for legislative and executive decision-making. Complete and up-to-date monitoring and fact-gathering tools are required for any responsible state planning operation (see CALIFORNIA TWO, pages 43, 44).

**8. Urge federal action.** We can urge that the federal government design all federal grants and loans to the state and local governments, including "revenue sharing," to serve and encourage strong state planning/budgeting operations, and comprehensive regional plans and budgets backed up by regional governments able to carry them out. Federal aid can thus become a partner in total regional improvement programs, and the federal government and the general public can at long last be assured that tens of billions of dollars collected annually from taxpayers across the nation do not continue to be used in ineffective, disconnected programs. (For example, in CALIFORNIA TWO, a Federal Conservation and Development Bank is designed as an effective financial resource for comprehensive regionwide improvement programs, page 53.)

In addition, Californians can openly and concertedly ask the federal government to institute other programs and policies essential to the well-being of the states. (These include, in the CALIFORNIA TWO narrative, a national income floor, national health insurance, national policies for settlement, population and resource use, and a variety of tax and fiscal reforms.)

**9. Make the commitment.** The California Tomorrow Plan is an attempt to post clear conditions of passage to survival with amenity. These conditions require that we change some of our ways of living and switch around some priorities on spending. They suggest that we must take certain risks—that to build the future, we must adjust the towering disparity between our expenditures for defense and those for domestic improvements; or that to protect the bright land of California, we risk inconvenience by forswearing the use of certain machines or products or poisons. They ask, above all, for a broad public commitment to compassionate, systematic, comprehensive planning —the kind which we have tried to exemplify in CALIFORNIA Two itself. We can, at long last, make such a commitment and, to win the future, we will.

# California Two policies— a summary

The California Tomorrow Plan describes two futures for the state: CALIFORNIA ONE and CALIFORNIA TWO. CALIFORNIA ONE, in which the quality of life becomes seriously impaired before the year 2000, is a logical consequence of today's methods of dealing with environmental and social disruptions. In CALIFORNIA ONE, problems are met, in general, through separate, disconnected programs. There is no cohesive strategy for solving them. CALIFORNIA TWO attempts to deal with disruptions in a systematic way through a process of comprehensive state and regional planning. As the chart on the following pages indicates, all programs and policies of CALIFORNIA TWO are based on central or driving policies. The driving policies, in turn, are addressed to underlying causes of disruption. The coordinated approach of CALIFORNIA TWO makes possible personal fulfillment within an amenable environment.

# California Two policies — a summary

| Some direct causes of disruption in California | Underlying causes of disruption | California Two driving policies |
| --- | --- | --- |

Obsolete governmental institutions

Inaccessibility to effective individual control

Overcontrol of individual action

Lack of individual political strength

1: PROVIDE POLITICAL STRENGTH

Distribution pattern of income, goods and services

Effect of tax structure

Lack of finance

Lack of individual economic strength

2: PROVIDE ECONOMIC STRENGTH

Little public control of destructive activities

Infrastructure location

Population growth

Damaging distribution of population

3: GUIDE SETTLEMENT

Population growth

Consumption practices

Limited resource supply

Effect of market system

Damaging patterns of resource consumption

4: GUIDE RESOURCE USE

| Components of California Two policies | Effects of policies on disruptions | | |
|---|---|---|---|
| | LAND | STRUCTURES | PEOPLE |
| State planning and budgeting combined under State Planning Council | Assures that all costs and benefits associated with alternative courses of action are considered in formation of policy decisions. Replaces uncoordinated, competitive programs of single-purpose agencies. | | |
| Comprehensive California State Plan prepared and annually updated. | Emerging problems, changing values and fresh approaches to solutions are recognized and regularly and systematically incorporated into official state policy. The plan serves as an effective contemporary guide for action. | | |
| Regional governments established to prepare and administer regional conservation and development plans and programs. | Provides sufficient jurisdiction and realistic fiscal base for problem solving. | | Makes government structure more accessible to public control. Allows greater individual and community participation in and control of government policies and programs in all areas of statewide concern, social as well as environmental. |
| Counties become municipalities; community councils established; campaign and election procedures reformed. | Assures recognition of local concerns and provides problem-solving methods which invite public participation. | | |
| Income floor established. | | | Alleviates poverty; provides means to enjoy amenities of California Two. |
| State guides economic development. | Encourages family farms. Employs youth in natural resource areas. | Provides housing and public facilities. | Creates jobs and wage sources. |
| Major assistance from Federal Conservation and Development Bank for comprehensive regional programs. | Assures grants and low-interest funds for open-space programs. | Assures grants and low-interest funds for development of housing and public facilities. | Well-planned programs make use of private as well as public financing. Taxpayers assured that money is efficiently used. |
| State zoning plan adopted. | Preserves agricultural land, open space, wildlife habitats. Conserves natural resources. | Guides urban growth and settlement patterns. | Assures beauty and life to cities and amenities to city dwellers; provides increased recreational opportunities. |
| State infrastructure plan adopted. | Prevents destructive patterns of land use. | Locates public facilities according to need. | Provides convenient, efficient public facilities and services. Generates jobs and salaries. |
| "California Standards" of amenity established. | Provides maximum open space and parklands for populace. | Ensures that structures of all kinds conform to standards of beauty, convenience, function and safety. | Guarantees that environmental quality becomes a major consideration in planning at all levels. |
| Zero population growth policy adopted. | Reduces demand for land and natural resources. | Slows increasing demands for housing and public facilities. | Permits existing populations a decent share of the goods, services and amenities of California. |
| Regulations and incentives established to guide resource use and encourage recycling. | Prevents exploitation and encourages wise use of land and resources. | Ensures that building programs are undertaken in accordance with wise resource use. | Maintains the life-support system upon which this and future generations depend. |

# A note about the editor

ALFRED HELLER is founder and president of California Tomorrow, a nonprofit educational organization dedicated to maintaining a beautiful and productive natural environment in California. The organization publishes the quarterly magazine, *Cry California*.

A native of California, Mr. Heller is a graduate of Stanford University. For several years he was publisher of the weekly *Nevada County Nugget*. He has served as a member of the California State Highway Commission. Author of numerous articles on environmental problems, Mr. Heller is also co-author, with Samuel E. Wood, of *California Going, Going . . .* and *The Phantom Cities of California*. In 1970 he received the Distinguished Service Award of the California Council, American Institute of Architects. He lives in Kentfield, Marin County, with his wife Ruth and their four daughters.

# Suggestions for further reading

The published literature that bears, in one way or another, on the subject matter of this book is virtually limitless. Readers who wish to pursue certain subjects further, such as public health, land use, or transportation, can begin with information sources closest at hand—for example, your public or school library.

Perhaps more than anything else, The California Tomorrow Plan is concerned with the planning process itself—how society can organize itself to solve its major problems. Books that present a more or less broad view of the planning process include:

ALTSHULER, ALAN, *The City Planning Process: A Political Analysis*, Cornell University, Ithaca, New York, 1965

HALL, PETER, *The World Cities*, McGraw-Hill Book Company, New York, 1966

MCHARG, IAN, *Design with Nature*, Natural History Press, Garden City, New York, 1969

Interesting examples or descriptions of actual public plans, reflecting social and economic as well as environmental concerns:

*State of Hawaii Land Use Districts and Regulations Review*, prepared by Eckbo, Dean, Austin & Williams for the State of Hawaii Land Use Commission, Honolulu, 1969

*General Plan for Lake Tahoe* and *Land Capabilities Map: Lake Tahoe Basin*, Tahoe Regional Planning Agency, South Lake Tahoe, California, 1972. The Lake Tahoe planning effort has been supported by a computer-assisted planning information system which is described in James E. Pepper, *An approach to environmental impact evaluation of land use plans and policy: the Tahoe basin planning information system*, Department of Landscape Architecture, University of California, Berkeley, 1972

*New York City Plan*, New York City Planning Department, 1970

*The South East Study: 1961-1981*, Ministry of Housing and Local Government, Her Majesty's Stationery Office, London, 1964

Among the many excellent publications which explore the world's environmental predicament are:

EHRLICH, PAUL R., AND EHRLICH, ANNE H., *Population, Resources, Environment: Issues in Human Ecology*, W. H. Freeman and Company, San Francisco, 1972

WILSON, CARROLL, editor, *Man's Impact on the Global Environment*, Study of Critical Environmental Problems, MIT Press, Cambridge, 1970

For a discussion of environmental issues from the standpoint of federal and state government, see:

*Environmental Quality*, first and second annual reports of the Council on Environmental Quality, U.S. Government Printing Office, Washington, D.C., 1970, 1971

*State of California Environmental Goals and Policies*, Office of Planning and Research, Governor's Office, Sacramento, 1972

*Progress Reports*, State of California Environmental Quality Study Council, Sacramento, 1970, 1971, 1972

One of the major issues addressed by The California Tomorrow Plan is the need for political-economic structures which can allow society to solve its most pressing problems. Books related to this subject include:

DAHL, ROBERT A., AND LINDBLOM, CHARLES E., *Economics, Politics and Welfare*, Harpers, New York, 1957

PERLOFF, HARVEY S., editor, *The Future of the U.S. Government: Toward the Year 2000*, commissioned by the American Academy of Arts and Sciences, George Braziller, Inc., New York, 1971

RODWIN, LLOYD, *Nations and Cities: A Comparison of Strategies for Urban Growth*, Houghton Mifflin Company, Boston, 1970

SCOTT, STANLEY, AND BOLLENS, JOHN C., *Governing a Metropolitan Region: The San Francisco Bay Area*, Institute of Governmental Studies, University of California, Berkeley, 1968

*Stockholm and Beyond*, Secretary of State's Advisory Committee, Department of State, Washington, D.C., 1972

STRONG, ANN LOUISE, *Planned Urban Environments*. Sweden, Finland, Israel, The Netherlands, France. Johns Hopkins Press, Baltimore, 1971

Shorter works dealing respectively with regional and federal responsibilities for protecting the quality of life include:

WHEATON, WILLIAM L. C., "Metro-Allocation Planning," *Journal of the American Institute of Planners*, March, 1967

WOOD, SAMUEL E., AND LEMBKE, DARYL, *The Federal Threats to the California Landscape*, California Tomorrow, San Francisco, 1967

# Index

In this index, 34f means separate references on pp. 34 and 35; 34ff means separate references on pp. 34, 35 and 36 only; 34-36 means a continuous discussion.
*Index prepared by Jeanne D. Kennedy*

health care in, 73–74, 80; transportation in, 80–82
Regional reserve zoning, 58f, 62, 70f, 78, 82
Regions, 46f, 71. *See also* Regional government
Regulatory commissions and agencies, 25, 45
Relief programs, 33, 78
Rent supplements, 32f
Resort developments, 11
Resource use: through Driving Policy 4, 39, 41–42, 44f, 57, 65–69, 87, 105, 110
Retraining programs, 16, 33
Rights-of-way, 68, 81
Riots, *see* Civil disorder
Rivers, 11, 13, 27f
Riverside County, 93
Roads, 12; costs of, 95f, 98. *See also* Highway system; Freeways
Robberies, 35
Rural areas: and automobiles, 13f; subdivision of, 29; health-care centers in, 74; assistance programs for, 77. *See also* Agricultural land

Sacramento: rapid-transit system in, 30
Salamander, Santa Cruz long-toed, 13
Salmon fisheries, 11, 29
Salts: buildup in land, 12, 28, 62
Salt marshes, 28
San Bernardino County, 93
San Diego: rapid-transit system in, 30, 52
San Fernando earthquake, 15
San Francisco, 15, 30, 72
San Francisco Bay: pollution of, 11f, 27
San Francisco Bay Area, 71, 91; air quality, 13; median income in, 15; rapid transit in, 30
San Joaquin Valley, 11f
San Jose, 95
San Mateo County, 49
Santa Barbara, 72–73
Santa Barbara County, 72–73
Santa Clara County, 70–71
Santa Cruz County, 72
Santa Cruz Mountains, 70
Schools, financing of, 16, 54, 81; "alternative," 16; construction of, 26; and employment, 33; as community centers, 63, 79
Security services, private, 35
Settlement: through Driving Policy 3, 39–42, 44f, 57–66, 73, 87, 105f, 110
Sewage, 13, 27
Sex education, 16
Sheep, Bighorn, 13

Shorelines, 11, 25, 59. *See also* Coastline
Siltation, 28f
Slurbs, 19
Smog, 13, 72, 93. *See also* Air pollution
Snowmobiles, 12
Soils: topsoil loss, 11f; salt buildup in, 12; depletion of, 18, 28, 57
Solar energy, 11, 67
Solid wastes, *see under* Wastes
Southern California: water sources in, 11; median income in, 15; fires in, 31–32; transport in, 82, 93–96
Southern California Rapid Transit District, 93–96
Southern Pacific, 72
Species, extinct and endangered, 12–13, 29
Stanford Research Institute, 95–96
State government, 21, 24–25, 56, 63, 89; funding by, 48f, 53, 55f, 99, 106; economy of, 51–52. *See also* California State Plan
State Planning Council, 39, 43–46, 51, 54, 66, 105
State Supreme Court, 16
Steelhead fisheries, 11, 29
Streams, 62; pollution of, 11, 29; siltation of, 28
Structures: as major-disruption category, 10, 14–15, 18–19, 40, 48, 88, 90
Suisun Marsh, 27
Surplus-commodity program, 17
Swimming, 27
Synanon, 67

Taxes, 84, 102, 106; income, 14f, 21, 32f, 51, 66, 68, 78, 83f, 106; gasoline, 14, 30; property, 16, 26, 55, 67; and land use, 26f, 67–68; and campaign contributions, 50; on automobiles, 67, 97; and oil depletion, 67, 97; and recycling, 68, 97
Teaching, compensatory, 16
Technological development, 21
Television: closed-circuit, 35; and elections, 50
Thermal pollution, 11, 27
Tidal energy, 11
Timber, 11f, 13, 59
Topsoil loss, 11f
Tract housing, 26, 32
Traffic congestion, 30
Trains, *see* Rail travel
Transit, public, 14, 25, 60, 81, 95; rapid, 13, 30, 52, 54, 80, 93–94, 96ff
Transportation, 14, 18, 75; non-polluting forms of, 61; in Santa Barbara, 72–73; for regions, 75, 80–82; in Los Angeles

area, 93–98. *See also by name*
Transportation Agency, 25
Trucking operators, 13

Unemployment, 16, 18, 78; compensation for, 33
Unions: and farm workers, 33
United States of America, 21. *See also* Federal government
U. S. Highway 101, 72
Universities, 16, 35
University of California: agricultural services of, 52; at Santa Barbara, 72; medical centers of, 74
Urban areas and urbanization, *see* Cities
Urban zone, 58f, 62, 70
Utilities, 9; public, 27, 57; costs, 92–93

Vehicles, *see* Motor vehicles
Venereal disease, 17
Ventura County, 93
Visual order, 14
Vocational training, 16
Voluntary associations: and regional planning, 26

Ward, Barbara, 6
Wastes: disposal of, 13f, 18, 25, 77, 83; solid, 14–15, 31, 68, 83; fees for dischargers of, 60–61; salvaged, 68
Water, 26, 54, 59, 77; pollution of, 10–14, 17f, 27, 29, 60–62; interbasin transfers of, 11, 27, 68, 83; groundwater, 11, 18; desalinization and recycling of, 11, 27, 68, 83; and agriculture, 12, 28, 52; recreational use of, 13, 17, 27; California Standards for, 61–62, 65, 83
Water Resources, Department of, 25
Watersheds, 12, 28, 91
Wilderness, 11–12, 17, 28–29
Wildlife habitats, 11, 13ff, 18, 29, 91
Wind energy, 11

Youth, 34; and unemployment, 16, 52
Zero population growth, 9, 21, 65–66
Zoning, 26, 44, 57–60, 65, 91; floodplain, 15, 31; and noise, 29; agricultural, 52, 55, 57–59, 62, 70, 77–78, 82, 91; conservation, 55, 58f, 61, 70, 77–78, 82; urban, 58f, 70, 82; regional reserve, 58f, 70, 82; and Santa Clara County, 70–71.

# Notes